Vendée
& La Rochelle

James Davey

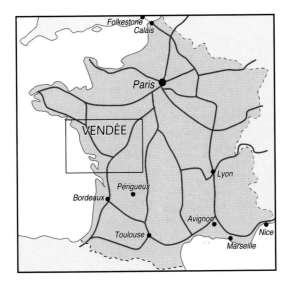

Dedication

To Joy, my wife,
whose powers of observation were so much better than mine,
and have led to the inclusion of many of the more interesting
features of this book.

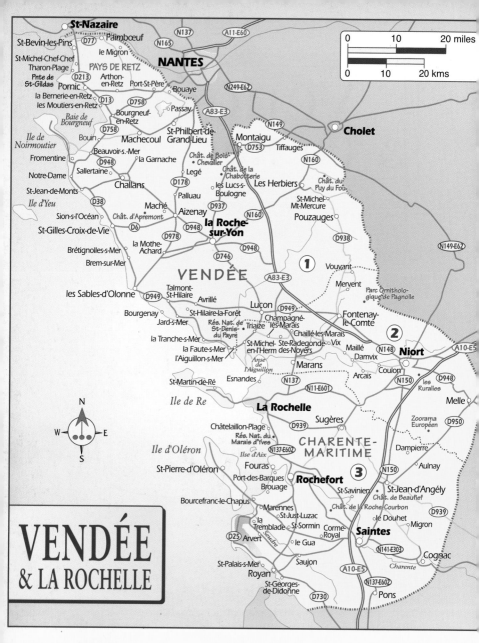
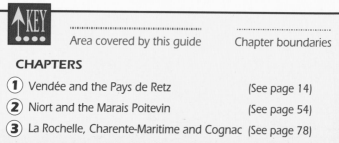

Vendée
& La Rochelle

James Davey

• AUTHOR'S TOP TIPS •

Whatever style of holiday you are taking there are four major attractions covered by this book that should not be missed:

- La Rochelle city and harbours in Charente Maritime.
- The miles of beautiful sandy beaches all down the coast and on the islands.
- The Puy du Fou theme park and Cinéscénie in the Vendée.
- The *Chais* of the Great Houses at Cognac.

There are many château and feudal castles to see, and of those described you should not miss:

- Château de la Roche-Courbon between Saintes and Rochefort.
- Château de la Gataudière near Marennes.
- Donjon at Niort.
- The best aquarium in the area is at La Rochelle including the Shark Room.

Recommended museums

- Musée du Nouveau Monde, La Rochelle.
- Musée Maritime, La Rochelle.
- Corderie Royale, Rochefort.

Introduction

With a weather pattern to rival the Mediterranean Coast and with over 2,400 hours of sunshine per year, you can be almost certain of fine weather for your holiday. There are all sorts of holidays available in the Vendée and in Charentes: seaside holidays at some of the most sophisticated resorts in France, with weather to match; holidays in a caravan or tent at the end of a long sand spit with only the sea and the marshes for company; *gîtes* (self-catering cottages) to rent and châteaux to stay in.

Then there are inland holidays in major towns, holidays on farms, at *chambres d'hôtes* (bed and breakfast), on camping sites where you can hire a caravan, or where you can take your own.

The French like to crowd their holidays into July and August when the weather is generally settled. But since there are many people about and prices tend to be higher, it follows you will have a more enjoyable time if you come early, May and June, or later, in September, when the weather is still excellent by our standards.

LET'S LOOK BACK A WHILE...

In an area like this that is so steeped in history, inevitably there are many references to past events. To get these in perspective and for more enjoyment of your holiday, these notes should be helpful, though you will find more detail in the text where needed. More information about the Religious Wars will be found in the section on the city of La Rochelle.

IN THE BEGINNING

Six or seven thousand years ago, the land was already settled by farmers of the New Stone Age. They used stone as their major tool material, though wood, bone and antler were in use for specialist purposes. Probably for religious reasons they raised large stones (technically called menhirs from the Celtic for 'long stone' and also called megaliths with a similar meaning) and built burial chambers for their

group, often on high ground near the sea.

During the Middle Ages, when their origin was not known, the French called them *Pierres Folles*, best translated as 'strange' or 'odd stones'. In the guide a number of these are visited, though for those with a keen interest in pre-history, the museum and grounds at Cairn, near St-Hilaire-le-Forêt in the Vendée, will be more than rewarding.

THE ROMANS

They had conquered Gaul (modern France and Belgium) by the beginning of the present era and had built up a network of roads joining their main towns. Saintes itself has many Roman remains, including its arena, its baths and the museum next to the Arc de Germanicus, a triumphal arch, now re-erected by the river Charente.

The Roman Empire broke up around 476AD, much as result of barbarian invasions, not least of which was by the Franks, invading over the Rhine. Within 20 years of their arrival, they had established their first dynasty, called the Merovingian after its founder Merovech, and remains of this time are so called.

THE MIDDLE AGES

These could equally have been called the Great Age of Pilgrimage. Of the many places to make a pilgrimage, that of St. James of Compostella was one of the most important. From the tenth century pilgrims came from all over Europe and collected in four main towns: Paris for those from northern Europe; Vezelay for Polish and German pilgrims; le Puy taking those from Austria, Hungary and further east, and Arles for those from Italy.

From these four points they made for the Pyrenees, crossing near the Bay of Biscay and continuing into northern Spain to Compostella. The actual routes through France were many, and as you visit towns, châteaux and churches you will find mention of the pilgrims or see the scallop shell, their symbol, carved into walls and above doors.

Many English and Scottish pilgrims preferred the sea voyage to the north Vendée landing at Bourgneuf, Bouin and Nantes and made their way south through Saintes, Parthenay and the small town of Palluau, where there is now a museum to the pilgrimage.

THE ENGLISH ARRIVE IN FORCE

In 1154 the English king Henry II married the richest woman in Christendom, Eleanor of Aquitaine, and with her came a dowry of all western France. This became Henry's Angevin Empire, based at Angers on the Loire, inland from Nantes.

A hundred years later, the French king had won back most of it, leaving only the area from Saintes and Angoulême south towards the Pyrenees in English hands. Power politics led to the disagreements intensifying, and the Hundred Years War broke out in 1337 lasting until 1453. English forces twice came close to gaining control of France but their resources were insufficient, and after continuous losses, by 1553 the only remaining English possession in France was Calais, and that was lost in 1558.

CATHOLIC AGAINST PROTESTANT

Barely having removed the English, France was once again plunged into war: this time with itself. Many parts of France, and particularly the area covered by this guide, had a considerable Protestant minority. The first Religious War from 1562 to 1598, had eradicated Protestants from France north of the Loire.

During the time of the Angevin Empire of Henry, La Rochelle was one of the English fiefs or strongholds, which in order to maintain their independence and rights, had played off the English and the French. Despite more persecution from the Catholic majority, many towns, including la Rochelle, retained their rights under the Edict of Nantes to garrison their towns, hold their own courts and guarantee their religion. A second Religious War started in 1621 and by 1629, the Protestants were thoroughly defeated and France was Catholic again.

PEACE AT LAST

France, now at peace internally, grew over the next 150 years to become the foremost power in Europe and foremost in science, war and arts. It was at this time that most aristocrats demolished their feudal castles to build less draughty and more luxurious châteaux, often re-using the old stones.

Louis XIV, called the Sun King, came to the throne in 1643. France was accurately mapped in sections at a scale of about 1.36 miles to the inch, the first country in the world to do so. Canals and other waterworks were built. French men of letters led the world in scientific discoveries. Unfortunately, France's military ambitions eroded the wealth she had built up and a series of financial crises led to the Revolution in 1789.

THE REVOLUTION

It left a significant mark on the region. The Vendéens carried out a long and bloody counter-revolution: those châteaux that were not burnt (eg. Château du Puy du Fou) were taken over by the state. Often they were sold off to non-aristocratic people (Château du Douhet), some owners managed to hold onto them and they have stayed in the same family ever since (Château de la Gataudière).

The Revolution was followed by the execution of the king and a persecution of the priests, the trigger that sparked the Vendéen Wars. The people, the church and the aristocrats in the Vendée and surrounding areas rose against the republicans. The Vendéens took as their emblem the double heart and cross on a white flag, becoming known as the 'whites', whilst the republicans were known as the 'blues' from their uniforms.

The war ebbed to and fro for the next four years, peace at times, war at others; atrocities were carried out by both sides, but especially by the blues. Finally the uprising was put down with great ferocity, the population being quite literally decimated; men, women and children were slaughtered in their thousands. Although the French are not at all proud of this episode in their history, they are making some amends today by building memorials, and through such events as the Cinéscénie at the Puy du Fou.

Continued on page 12...

9

Above: Shopping in La-Tranche-sur-Mer

Left: Moulin de Rairé, Sallertaine

Below: Sunflowers

Above: Flowers

Right: Grapes for Cognac

Below: Roadside Flea Market

WORLD WAR II

There are a number of reminders of World War II. In the north of the region at the Pointe de St-Gildas you can see the remains of the many gun emplacements forming part of Germany's Atlantic Wall. Further south, in the Forêt de la Coubre near Royan, are strong points hidden amongst the trees. However it was on the Islands of Ré and Oléron and particularly at Royan itself that the Germans resisted the Allies to the bitter end. Royan was destroyed by allied bombing, and there is a good museum to this at le Gua, 11 miles (18km) north of the town.

TO HELP YOU GET AROUND

French Tourist Offices are called by a variety of names: Office de Tourism is gaining popularity at the moment, though you will find Syndicat d'Initiative, Bureau de Tourism, OTSI, or just SI. In the guide they are always called Tourist Office for simplicity. The largest offices are open all day in the summer and always have English speakers in attendance. The next grade are usually open all day, though many will close from noon to 2pm, and will probably have English speaking staff. The smallest can often take three hours for lunch, not opening until three o'clock or later! You are unlikely to find English spoken here.

THE REGION

The Vendée and Charente are areas that have been fought over for a thousand years and more, and there are numerous castles and châteaux. The medieval castles here are usually referred to as feudal castles, following French convention. In many instances outer walls have disappeared leaving only the keep, often called a *donjon* in French, which is used in the guide.

There are hundreds of miles of coast, and much of this is sandy beach. There are fens that were once bays till they silted up, and here wildlife abounds. Ten of the many special nature reserves have been highlighted in their own section, Pôles Nature.

Most of the seaside towns are attractive, some like Pornic in the north, particularly so. Inland though is where you will find interesting small towns, each with their own character. Many have been bypassed by the traffic and form small oases of quiet, whereas others are still waiting.

The further inland you go the less tourists are catered for, and to many this is a blessing. Nevertheless wherever you go you will find the road network to be fast and generally efficient. However on holiday not everyone wants to travel at breakneck speed and the major N and D prefixed roads are best avoided. On Michelin maps you can see the yellow roads that are useful for taking a more sedate pace.

For more detailed getting around, and you will need this to get to many of the recommended places, use the IGN (French 'Ordnance Survey') maps at a scale of 1 cm to 1km, which is awkwardly, about 4 miles to $2^1/_2$ inches.

For getting round the islands by car or cycle each has an even larger scale of map at 1:25000, or about $2^1/_2$ inches to the mile, similar to our own Explorer maps by Ordnance Survey. Further information on maps will be found in the Fact File.

• THREE SHOPS •

Where you can buy that present that is just a little different.

Ismail Poterie at Aizenay.

Here, as you leave the town for la Roche-sur-Yon, craftsman Ismail Kus has set up an interesting pottery. Ismail came originally from Turkey and first set up his business in Mouilleron-en-Pareds, 21miles (35km) the other side of la Roche. Ten years ago came the chance of these bigger premises, and his work is on display outside and in the 'Aladdin's cave' of his basement. He is established selling to other local businesses as well as retail sales here. Outside are the garden terra-cotta pots in all shapes and sizes, and inside are majolica designs and special Turkish models with raised relief. You can ask him too about the lessons he offers in his craft.

Marie-Claire Daubert has joined him. Her talents include specialising in cut-out pottery which she makes, amongst other things, into lamps of all shapes and sizes: table lamps, ceiling lamps, side lamps for the house as well as the garden. Ask her too, about her dishes for pot-pourri, you'll be in for a pleasant surprise.

☎ 05 51 48 32 08.

La Vannerie at Notre-Dame-de-Monts.

Vannerie means wicker-work, and in here you will find plenty of that. But not just baskets and chairs and tables, there are giant fans and butterflies too. Then the less exotic presents include Vendéen products to eat and drink, and every manner of gift and souvenir. Make sure you go upstairs to the first and second floors, and ask to see the monastery table that weighs a quarter of a tonne. And if that is not enough, see the huge head carved in elm. Not only is it hollow but it is many centuries old, how many you can only guess at! La Vannerie is on the main Route de la Barre, D38, at Notre-Dame-de-Monts, and they have another shop at Notre-Dame-de-Riez, $18^1/_2$ miles (30km) away. This is in an old farm-house on the banks of the River Vie, that they have completely renovated.

☎ 05 51 58 80 39.

Au Plaisir d'Offrir at La Cotinière

Not to be missed is the shop *Au Plaisir d'Offrir*, It's a Pleasure to Offer, facing the port at la Cotinière. Amongst all the garish seaside gifts is the speciality of the house – hundreds of model boats. In fact they have models from 2in (5cm) long for a few francs to elaborate models of Oléronais fishing boats at over a thousand francs. There are hundreds of different models and you cannot fail to find a present here for your nautical friends! La Cotinière is on the south-west coast of the Ile d'Oléron.

Vendée and the Pays de Retz

1

The Vendée is perhaps best known for its shining, soft sandy beaches. The almost unbroken 70 miles (110km) of beautiful beach stretching from St-Brevin-les-Pins, past the Ile de Noirmoutier to La Faute-sur-Mer is backed by pine woods in many places, and by seaside towns in others. However the Vendée is not all beach, there are many other Vendées coming together and forming a wonderful holiday area. They start in the north east at the high hills of the Collines Vendéennes and spread across the slightly undulating countryside to the flat coastal areas and those sandy beaches.

In the flat west of the Vendée you have the chance to see some remarkable evening skies coming in on the breeze. Everything you can wish for is here: majestic clouds reflecting the setting sun off their peaks; beams striking down to the ground; rays piercing even higher; the golden glow of sunset peeking at you from dark clouds. And what finer way to spend your evening,

sitting with a bottle of Vendéen Gros Plant white wine,and enjoying the beauty of the sun going down?

The Department is establishing a network of cycle tracks along the coast from the north of the Ile de Noirmoutier to les Sables-d'Olonne, and from La Tranche-sur-Mer right into the Marais Poitevin. Much of it is available now, but it is an ongoing programme of off-road tracks and green-marked lanes on roads. Get the leaflet *'Circuits de Randonnées à Vélo en Vendée'*, Cycle rides in the Vendée, from any tourist office.

The two isles of Noirmoutier and Yeu are a total contrast to each other. Noirmoutier is very flat, much of it below high water mark, and of all the islands off the French coast, is the only one that has always been connected to the mainland by road, albeit at low water. Yeu on the other hand, is higher and rocky and with the charm of a small isle that likes to show its fierce independence from the mainland.

On the southern banks of the Loire Estuary lies the **Pays de Retz**. Although it runs into the Vendée, it is historically part of Brittany, and today in the Department of Loire Atlantique. As with the Vendée it has much to offer the holidaymaker from its sandy beaches, theme parks and megalithic monuments to its river- and lake-side bird-watching.

So here is a land of sun, sand, water and grass. Let's see what it is has to offer.

PAYS DE RETZ

E nter Pornic from the junction of the D213, La Route Bleue, and the D751. At the bottom of the hill are the railway station and the Tourist Office. There is plenty of free parking all around this, the most picturesque of the ports between the Loire and the Gironde.

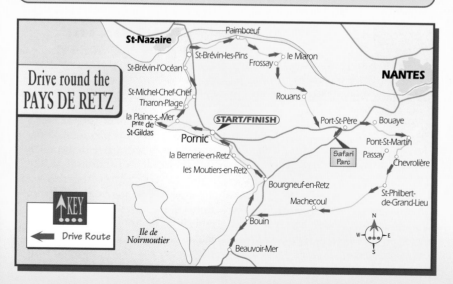

Drive round the **PAYS DE RETZ**

The fishing port is right by the bridge and just beyond is the medieval town reaching up the hill behind, where most of the old fishermen's houses are now shops. The Casino is along the port towards the château, not open to the public, and above is the Place de la Terrasse, with enchanting views over both the château and the town.

Below the château is the **Plage du Château**, no swimming allowed, one of twelve sandy beaches along the coast, and this is the starting point for a walk along the **Corniche de la Noëveillard** to the marina just over half a mile (1km) away, and the golf course above.

You can continue past the marina along the top of the low cliffs past three beaches to the **Plage du Porteau**, where you turn inland and follow the signs back through Ste-Marie to Pornic making the walk 5 miles (8km). At the same Plage are the signs to the interesting **Dolmen des Mousseaux**, now completely restored, with its double passage and stones that are staged in sizes, making it both a tomb and a memorial to the neolithic farmers who originally erected it some 5,000 years ago.

On the other side of the estuary the **Corniche de Gourmallon** is a shorter walk of 2 miles (3km) above the cliffs past the **Anse aux Lapins** beach, also no bathing, to the **Plage de la Source** and straight back along the road to Pornic harbour. Boats leave the Môle for Ile de Noirmoutier, for sea trips and for fishing.

Nearby, parts of the wild west come to life at the **Bison Ranch**. Here in the depths of the country covered wagons, cavalry tents, tepees, and an Indian reservation can be found as well as an Auberge Bar, a children's play area and a zoo of small animals.

The highlight of the visit is the tour round the 55 acre (23 hectare) farm by horse drawn covered wagon with the owner himself, who speaks a little English, giving a commentary. Like all the farms with exotic beasts here, the visit is almost incidental to the main business of raising them for food.

The ride takes you past the corral where the beasts are selected for weighing and slaughter, then on to see the dominant male with his six wives and calves born in February. Back at the ranch, as it were, you can buy various pig and bison products, or if you prefer, eat them in the restaurant. The visit alone should take no more than 45 minutes an hour, though as always, allow for queues in the high season.

A drive round this varied peninsular will take a day, though you must allow extra time for stops at any of the beautiful beaches, and your visit to the **Planète Sauvage – Safari Africain**.

TOUR OF THE PAYS DE RETZ

Leave Pornic on the D13 for **Plaine-sur-Mer** and **Pointe de St-Gildas**. Right at the end of the road at the Pointe, you can park for the viewing table to see the panorama from the bridge to St Nazaire in the north and to Ile de Noirmoutier in the south. In very clear weather it is just possible to see the islands off the south Brittany coast. The viewing table is on the top of one of the very many German gun emplacements here from the World War II, built to protect the Loire Estuary.

Opposite the shops and restaurant is sheltered mooring for pleasure boats and an 880yd (800m) jetty. The foreshore is delightfully rocky around the Pointe, but further on past the viewing table is the **Anse du Sud** with its small sandy beach.

Take the road back to la Plaine-sur-Mer, and turn north to **Tharon-Plage** the most southerly resort on the 8$^1/_2$ miles (14km) beach that extends to the mouth of the Loire at **le Nez-de-Chien.** Tharon-Plage is followed by **St-Michel-Chef-Chef, St-Brevin-l'Océan,** and **St-Brevin-les-Pins.** Tharon-Plage is probably the nicest of the sandy beaches here with good access and parking, though little in the way of services. The beach faces west and runs into that of St-Michel-Chef-Chef, which acts as the commercial nucleus.

St-Brevin-l'Océan has a wide flat sandy beach approached along pine lined and scented roads. There is a water toboggan in season. St-Brevin-les-Pins has a large beach at low tide though quite small at high. There is a good shopping area 440yd (400m) inland with a market.

At the Nez-de-Chien in **Mindin**, is the Maritime Museum in an old fort and further round towards the bridge to St-Nazaire, the Tourist Office has a photographic exhibition showing the construction of the bridge. Take the road to **Paimboeuf** built on an 'island' of hard stone gneiss, between the marshes and the River Loire.

Drive into the town along the Rue de l'Eglise and visit the church of St Louis in neobyzantine style. Round at the old dock area, the town fronts the River Loire, and there are many attractive houses facing the river. In the town's narrow streets you will find the Tourist Office. Further along the docks, now used by anglers and pleasure boats, there are still the old rails that carried the dockside cranes and the railway trucks.

Sit quietly on a hot afternoon, and you may hear the ghosts of the dock workers unloading ship after ship from America! More or less opposite to you is the refinery at **Donges**, and passing up and down the river are tugs bringing larger boats down from Nantes, petrol barges taking fuel up river, and fishing boats returning with their catch.

Leave by the Nantes road and in 4 miles (6km) turn off left for **le Migron**. At the heart of the village turn left again to the old **Lower Loire Maritime Canal**, at the Rue du Pont Tournant, Swing Bridge Street. The bridge is no longer there, but canal buffs will be pleased to see the stone pivot and abutments.

Drive beside the canal and cross the narrow bridge. Drive cautiously along the 1$^1/_2$ mile (2km) to the river, not because it is dangerous in any way, but because round almost any bend you will be close to flocks of marsh birds eagerly feeding: herons, spoonbills, egrets, avocets and

Changing times Paimboeuf grew up as a fishing town, then 200 years ago when the Atlantic trade grew it became the outer port for Nantes. In fact, during the Revolution in 1793, its population was 9,000, against that of St Nazaire across the river at 700. Since then things have changed somewhat!

moorhens to name but a few, and in the early autumn, even more migrants are stocking up for their long flight south. At the Loire, try to ignore the power station opposite, and look on the tranquil river, the fishermen's boats, the reeds and the wildlife.

From le Migron, with its nice little restaurant, make your way back through Frossay, to the main road and pick up the signs for Rouans and the **Planète Sauvage**. Established only in 1992 this huge theme park, also called Safari Africain, is of 240 acres (100 hectares) and contains some 1,500 animals in family groups. The tour of 6.2 miles (10 km), taking about 2 hours, goes through savannah-like enclosures surrounded by fences, many painted to give an African atmosphere.

To the relief of many parents a third the way round are refresh-ments and toilets and the chance for youngsters to walk among African farm animals.

Most of the important African animals are here, including white rhinoceros, black bears, lions and tigers (!) and the antelopes and zebras who are so friendly they will come to your car for titbits. Like all wildlife parks there are plenty of photo opportunities. Not all the animals are African, since the tigers and rhesus monkeys come from Asia... but then who's complaining, it's a good day out. At the end is a picnic area with a dozen or so tables and plenty of grass.

Go into the Village where there are a number of restaurants and bars and other exhibition houses, including some for spices and reptiles and a small zoo of miniature animals and the Monkey Forest.

However, the main feature here is the Cité Marine with performances by seals and dolphins daily in giant pools. You can walk under the pools to see the animals in the premier European Centre for the Rehabilitation of Marine Mammals (CERMAM), where the dolphins can recuperate in a step towards liberty and seals and porpoises found stranded on beaches can recover.

INLAND FROM PORNIC

Leave the Safari Africain for Nantes and 1 mile (1.5km) after Bouaye turn right to Pont-St-Martin and La-Chevrolière, then onto **Passay** and the **Observatoire**. Here you are on the banks of the **Lac de Grand-Lieu** formed in a huge depression in the land. Sixteen hundred years ago ships could pass right into the lake from the River Loire and discharge

Seals in the Cité Marine, Planète Sauvage

Above: White Rino at Planéte Sauvage

Right: Bison Ranch

Below: Fisherman, Lac de Grand-Lieu

their cargo at the southern end.

Gradually the lake has silted up, more lately with man's 'helpful hand', and what was once lake is now farm land, and what is now sometimes lake, is reed beds. In the winter the free water of the lake can cover as much as 20,000 acres (8,000 hectares), while in summer it falls to half that. Just to the north of Passay the River Ognon flows into the lake, and to the south, at St-Philbert-de-Grand-Lieu, is the river Boulogne.

Rare birds

From time immemorial, the Lac de Grand-Lieu has been fished, but with less and less water there are fewer fish, and with much of the better parts made into conservation areas, there are only fifteen professional fishermen left. The lake is on the Atlantic migration routes for birds and plays host to some 200 species including ducks, grebes, rails, geese, snipe and teal. The heron, and the rare white spoonbill still use the lake for nesting. Even though it is a birdwatchers' paradise, many birds keep to the middle of the lake.

At Passay drive right to the end of the road, past the fishermen's black boats drawn up on the shore and on to the next beach where you will find a multitude of birds all within 100 yards (90m) of you. Binoculars are helpful. When you have had your fill return to the village and the Observatoire. The museum here shows life in days past in photographs, examples of fishermen's boats with both sails and outboard motors, the special style of nets, and an aquarium of the fish from the lake. At the top of the tower two powerful telescopes enable you to see right into the middle of the lake. Regular birdwatchers can identify the birds at this distance, and for those of us less knowledgeable, the special video transmission direct from the lake will be of interest.

Go to **St-Philbert-de-Grand-Lieu** with its nice park and a stroll along the river. The Tourist Office sells tickets to the **Maison du Lac**, the Abbey next door and for rowing boat hire on the River Boulogne.

The Maison du Lac is remarkable for its exhibition of 225 species of bird that either nest or pass through the lake. Here also is an audio-visual presentation of the flora and fauna and the same video transmission direct from the lake as at the Observatoire.

The spectacular bronze at St-Philbert-de-Grand-Lieu

General Louis Juchault de la Moricière, a local son, defeated one Abd el Kader in 1847. On this bronze, not only is Louis in full battle cry, but he is supported by his batman and a charming, almost naked lady; then at the back, the decisive moments of Abd el Kader's defeat.

This is a statue not to be missed, but one feels Louis may have sat happier fighting his eternal battle in Nantes or Paris. Louis was famous during the colonization of Algeria, and in 1962 when it became independent, the bronze came back to St-Philbert.

Next door is the old Abbey built in the ninth century under Charlemagne and is remarkable for both its great age and its attractive interior arches, with the alternate use of tile and stone.

Leave St-Philbert for Machecoul 9 miles (15km) along the fast D117. **Machecoul** has a reputation blotted in the distant past by a child murderer, and retrieved in the last century by Séguin, the producers of Fine Bretagne brandy! The twin steeples of the church are visible for some miles across the flat Marais Breton marshes immediately to the west of the town. You can find the Tourist Office between the church and the market hall where the Rue du Marché, the main shopping street starts.

By the railway station, but on the other side of the tracks, in the aptly named Boulevard St Rémy, are the offices and warehouses of Séguin. Séguin is owned by Rémy Martin but operate in quite a different way to their parent. Unlike the big cognac houses of Cognac itself, Séguin buy in their eau-de-vie from commercial distillers, and use their skills to age and blend in their own style.

If you intend going to Cognac to visit the *chais* there, don't avoid the visit here, as it is complementary to the others. The visit is introduced by a slide presentation with an En-glish commentary, followed by a tour of the *chais*. The vats in which the brandy is maturing, one as large as 8,450 gallons (38,000 lt) each have a descriptive panel in English. At the end you can taste and buy their many products.

BEAUVOIR TO PORNIC

From Machecoul take the D59 along the edge of the Marais Breton to Bouin and go south on the D758 to **Beauvoir-sur-Mer** where the Tourist Office serving both Beauvoir and Bouin is in the main street. It is a busy little town supporting a large rural and fishing population. The Tourist Office will give you information about salt and oyster production, which interestingly have replaced the frog fishing industry!

Leave the town by the D948 for the **Passage du Gois**, the ancient causeway to the Ile de Noirmoutier, from the local dialect word *goiser*, to paddle. There are plenty of notices giving the day's information about the permitted times to cross to Noirmoutier by the Passage. On the way call at a craftsman copper beater's shop in an old barn beside the road and next to one of the marsh ponds.

Continued on page 24...

Oysters

Oysters are readily available and, should you not have a favourite recipe, here are two favoured by local restaurants:

Fisherman's Oysters (*Huîtres à la façon du Pecheur*)

Enough for 4
You will need: 24 large Vendéen oysters, 400g *pain de mie* (similar to a small British white loaf), 100g *crème fleurette*, 20g butter, a bunch of chervil, salt and pepper.

Open the oysters, straining the juice through a fine mesh and put aside. Remove the oysters gently from their shells. Slice the bread and cut into 24 fancy shapes. Toast them. Put the oysters into a frying pan with a little of the butter and cook for a few minutes. Prepare the sauce by slightly reducing the juice, adding the *creme fleurette* and whisking in the butter. Put the oysters onto the toast, 5 or 6 to the plate, cover with the sauce. Garnish with chervil and serve.

Oysters in Shallot and Parsley Butter (*Huîtres au Four*)

Enough for 4
You will need: 24 large Vendéen oysters, 100g of butter, shallots, chopped parsley, salt and pepper, crispy bread crumbs.

Carefully open the oysters, and keep the juice. Lightly clean the shells and return the oysters and juice. Chop the shallots and parsley finely then mix with the butter to give an even paste. Add salt (lightly) and pepper and spread each oyster with the butter. Sprinkle with the bread crumbs and cook for a few minutes in the oven. Serve on a bed of sea salt and with lemon wedges, garnished with parsley and lemon rind.

Brioche

Brioche is a yeast-based bread, similar to a Sally Lunn Bun, and rich in eggs and butter. It is popular in the Vendée being eaten at any time of day. It is served in almost any suitable way: for example with butter, jam or cream as we might eat bread, or as a desert with apple purée and cream or yoghurt. The manufactured variety is often very dry, and the cheaper pre-packed types are not recommended. Brioche is usually made as loaves or plaited, though you can make them in any shape that takes your fancy. To make a nice brioche use this recipe.

You will need: 100ml milk, 100g butter or margarine, 75g sugar, half teaspoon salt, 3 tablespoons warm water, 10g baker's yeast or 2 teaspoons dry, 1 egg yolk beaten, 1 egg white, 3 more whole eggs, 375g flour, 1 tablespoon sugar.

Scald the milk, cool to lukewarm. Cream the margarine or butter and gradually add 75g sugar and the salt. Measure warm water into a bowl, sprinkle or crumble yeast, stir until dissolved. Stir in lukewarm milk and creamed mixture. Add beaten egg yolk, beaten eggs and flour, beat till smooth. Cover and let rise in a warm place for 2 hours or until doubled.

Stir down, beat thoroughly, cover tightly and store in refrigerator overnight. Stir down and turn out onto floured board. Put into a loaf tin, or plaited onto a baking sheet, or divided into individual buns (makes 16). Let rise in a warm place for an hour or until doubled. Brush with egg white and bake in a moderate oven, 190 °C, mark 5, for 20 minutes.

Chabichou du Poitou – The goat's cheese

One of the oldest cheeses in France, it has an AOC *(appellation d'origine controlée)* and must be made from goats' milk originating in an exactly defined area of the limestones of Poitou, and with a fat content of 45 per cent. Each cheese weighs around 150g and is shaped like a little cone 5 to 8 cm tall. It is ivory coloured with a soft texture and covered in a white crust. It can be eaten young (3 weeks), mature (6 weeks) or dry (2 months). It is very popular with connoisseurs and the public alike.

Mothais sur Feuille

Made into a disc 10 to 12cm diameter and 2.5cm high, it weighs 180 to 220g and it is normally placed on large chestnut or plane tree leaves at table. When it is three months old it can be eaten on its own, or when lightly grilled mixed in a salad. It is particularly favoured by gourmets – and they say, by gourmands too.

Chèvre en Boîte

At the beginning of the century Mothais sur Feuille was placed in small round boxes to make it easier to send to other parts of France. Slightly smaller in size to the locally sold cheese, it has a crust that reddens a little with age, and is best eaten at 8 weeks.

This is a recipe for using both the goats' cheese and some of the excellent fish available in the region.

Filets of Sole Chabichou

For two people. You will need: 4 fillets of sole, half a *chabichou*, 200cl of *fumêt de poisson*, *crème fraîche*, 2 shallots, chives for snipping, salt, pepper.

Salt and pepper the fillets, spread half the quantity of the *chabichou* over them with a fork. Roll the fillets and hold each together with two cocktail sticks. Cover the fillets with the *fumêt de poisson* and cook in the oven at 210 °C for a good 10 minutes, remove them and keep hot. Now, braise the finely chopped shallots and mix the cooking juices; let it reduce and incorporate the *crème fraîche* and the rest of the *chabichou* chopped into large dice. Cook for 2 minutes and liquidise in a mixer. Remove the cocktail sticks from the sole, cover with the sauce and serve.

Mussels

La Mouclade:

This simple dish is served in most restaurants, enjoyed by gastronomes as well as being cooked on many campsites in the area.

2kgs mussels, 4 onions, 1 soup spoon of flour, 100g fresh cream, white wine, 2 or 3 eggs, bouquet garni, butter, pepper, garlic.

Wash the mussels, add wine and bouquet garni. Heat on a high flame until the mussels open, discarding those that have not. In another pan brown the onions and add the flour. Thicken with the 'juice' from the mussels. Mix the egg yolks and cream, garlic and pepper, then add to mussels and serve.

Fish farm

Just a little further, and 1¹⁄₂ miles (2.5km) off to the left is a sea bass farm. They only open for very limited hours in the evening: the best time to see both the fish and the workings of the farm. The owners have developed the 25 acres (10 hectares) of salt marsh right by their home as a fish farm. A channel brings the tide to the ponds twice each day and with it food for the sea bass, as well as other fish including dory and eels. It takes four years for a bass to go from egg to a 1lb (500gm) fish, reflected in the high price they fetch.

Drive on towards the causeway where, despite the strong words of advice on the notice board about when not to attempt the crossing, there seems to be always someone prepared to risk a wetting. Every year the Gois is the host to a race, *Les Foulées du Gois*, Strides across the Gois, where the competitors race against the tide. Cross if you wish then go back to Beavoir and on to Bouin.

Bouin is on a former island when the present marshes were the Bay of Bourgneuf, and it is indeed still called Bouin Island. The town has had a history of disasters that must make the present inhabitants glad they are living in the twenty-first century.

In the first place it lay on the border of the two powerful and aggressive Duchies of Brittany and Poitou, who continually fought over it. As if this wasn't enough, it was flooded more than fifteen times in seven centuries, yet the town and fortifications were rebuilt each time. As a result, the church was fortified by the townspeople; the Duke of Poitou built the castle; and the Duke of Brittany built his fort, the Pavillion. Here you can to go up the church tower for a view across the marshes, the coast and the Ile de Noirmoutier to the west with the coast of Retz to the north.

Take the D118 towards Bourgneuf-en-Retz across the wild marshes. This narrow road, barely two cars wide, twists and turns through the salt marshes, with deep ditches on either side, and a depth of water that depends on the state of the tide. Watch for the wild life and two or three small herds of curiously coloured cattle. Cross the cobbled bridge that is wide enough for most cars, actually 6ft 10in (2.1m) wide, though a new bridge is planned, and go left to **Port-du-Collet** picking up the road signed Pornic par Côte.

On through **les Moutiers-en-Retz** and the bigger **la Bernerie-en-Retz** with the holiday makers in its main street spilling off the pavements almost under your wheels. Look above the shop façades to a wide variety of interesting and contrasting architecture.

Both les Moutiers and la Bernerie have sandy beaches, though at low tide the former becomes muddy and the latter goes to rocks and pebbles. On the way now to Pornic, there are two small beaches, **Plage de la Fontaine Breton**, sandy away from the top of the tide, and the more easily accessible though more rocky, **Plage de la Joselière**. Both give you a chance to stretch your legs and walk to their dolmens each only 440yd (400m) away to the left. Drive into Pornic to finish the drive.

A selection of markets in this area

Tuesday: Paimboeuf. St-Père-en-Retz, Tharon
Wednesday: Machecoul, Savenay
Thursday: Bouaye, Frossay
Friday: St-Sébastien, Paimboef, Tharon
Saturday: Tharon, Le Péllerin, La Chabossière
Sunday: Frossay, St-Père-en-Retz, St-Philbert-Grand-Lieu

Machecoul also on the first and third Tuesday and Sunday.

Places to Visit

Pays de Retz

LA FRAISERIE
Pornic
In the north part of the town off the D86.
Products based on strawberries are made here. Free factory tour and tasting. Jams, syrups, sweets, alcoholic drinks and punnets of strawberries on sale.
☎ 02 40 82 08 21.
Open: July and August, Monday to Thursday 2pm-5.30pm.

RANCHE DES BISONS
Arthon
Take the D751 towards Arthon-en-Retz and follow the signs to the Ranch des Bisons 9 miles (14km) away.
☎ 02 40 84 86 67
Open: 2pm-7pm June-end September. Not Monday.

SAFARI AFRICAIN — PLANÈTE SAUVAGE
Port-Saint-Père
Allow at least four hours, and probably the whole day, for your visit.
☎ 02 40 04 82 82
Open: February to November from 10am; in low season till 4pm, June July August till 5.30pm. Village closes at 9pm in summer.

OBSERVATOIRE
Passay
☎ 02 41 13 36 46.
Open: every day 10am-noon, 3pm-6.30pm.

VENDÉE COAST

There are over 60 miles (100km) of beautiful fine sandy beach stretching from the Ile de Noirmoutier in the north to la Faute-sur-Mer in the south, backed for the most part by resorts or by publicly owned pine forests. From the north, the three main resorts in the Côte-de-Monts are La Barre-de-Monts, Notre-Dame-de-Monts, and St-Jean-de-Monts. At Sion the rocks come down to the sea and form the 2 miles (3km) of the Corniche Vendéenne, then round the corner is the attractive fishing town and resort of St-Gilles-Croix-de-Vie lying at the mouth of the River Vie.

Noirmoutier-en-l'Ile Harbour

On south past the rocky coast at Brétignolles-sur-Mer is the large resort and fishing port of Les Sables-d'Olonne. More rocky coast interspersed with sandy coves leads to la Tranche-sur-Mer and its 13km, 8 miles, of beaches and on to the southernmost resort of la Faute-sur-Mer. Every town has its share of hotels, apartments and *gîtes*, but it is overall a caravanning and camping area with more sites per ten square kilometres than any other part of western France.

ILE DE NOIRMOUTIER

The **Ile de Noirmoutier** is the most northerly of the four main islands between the Loire and the Gironde. The easiest, though not the most exciting way onto the island is over the modern bridge, toll free since July 1994. A dual carriage way runs up the spine of the island and where it and the Passage-du-Gois road meet, is the main Tourist Office, set back on the right with its own parking area.

The island's main industries are fishing including oysters and mussels, salt harvesting, agriculture and tourism. Early in the year, in February and March, mimosa is cut and sent all over France. Fishing is declining, in common with the rest of Europe, and tourism is rapidly becoming the island's most important revenue producer. The main fishing port is l'Herbaudière and you can see the salt pans best outside Noirmoutier-en-l'Ile, the main town.

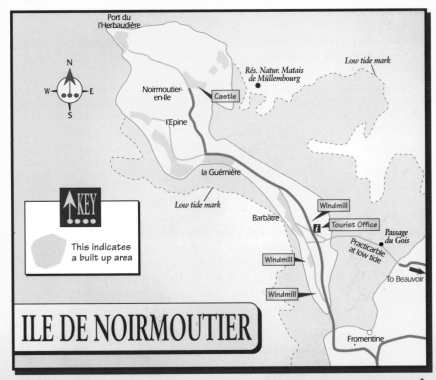

Pollution-free travel

You are encouraged to travel about the island by bike or on foot, with cycles available for hire all over the island. However with no network of cycle paths the dual carriageway, a 110kph road, must be used to get from one end of the island to the other. On the other hand the Tourist Office have prepared an attractive leaflet *Les Balades Insulaires*, Island Rambles, with 6 walks covering all parts of the island from 3 to $8\frac{1}{2}$ miles (4.5 to 14km).

Take the road opposite the Tourist Office to **Barbâtre**, a village now almost completely given over to holiday cottages and camping sites. The pantiled and whitewashed cottages and shops still retain all the old world charm and the market is held every Wednesday in the Place du Marché. A number of roads lead to the long south-west facing beach, though parking can be difficult. Houses and a couple of disused windmills crown the summits of the dunes about 220yd (200m) back from the beach giving a wide open space for horse riding, and games playing.

The next village on the western side of the island is **la Guérnière**, and a twist of the coast allows it to face due south. The church is surrounded by shops, with the market on Thursdays, and another on Sundays in July and August behind the Mairie. Here also is the **Musée des Traditions de l'Ile**. The beach is below a small esplanade, and at low tide there are sections of rocks with crabs and shrimps to collect with the locals.

The beach continues northwards for two miles to **l'Epine**, another holiday village with its market on Saturdays. Use the minor road across the salt marshes to **Noirmoutier-en-l'Ile** and as it twists and turns between the salt pans, you can often see a marsh harrier hovering over its prey.

Noirmoutier-en-l'Ile is the island's principal town with the main supermarket, and the best shopping area. This nestles to one side of the castle and is a network of narrow streets thronged with shoppers, buying clothes, seafood, holiday gifts both cheap and dear, and others just sitting passing the time in cafés. An engaging part of the shopping area is Place Saint Louis facing the port, an ideal place to watch the fishing boats come and go over a coffee and *crêpe*.

The Château, built 500 years ago, is a well-maintained feudal castle. From the roof of the *donjon* (keep) are magnificent views over the island and in clear weather you can see La Baule to the north and the Ile de Yeu in the south. On the ground floor of the *donjon* is shown the history of the Vendéen wars including the gruesome chair in which General d'Elbée was shot, on the first floor a maritime exhibition, and on the second and third, fine arts. In the Governor's *Logis* is an exhibition of English lustreware.

In the church of St Philbert, the same saint commemorated at St-Philbert-de-Grand-Lieu above, is the crypt of the ninth century dedicated to the Saint Philbert himself, and on either side of the choir are two sumptuous baroque altars.

Across the dock, in a former warehouse is **Sealand Aquarium,** ingeniously built around a large tank, open to the sky and containing the seals. As you walk round the several levels you have a different view of them swimming and diving. Flanking it are many tanks containing Mediterranean and tropical fish as well as local specimens including small sharks.

Local Museums

Further along the same side of the wharf is the **Musée de Sel**, Salt Museum, in an old Salt Warehouse and run by the Cooperative de Sel. Here are illustrations and diagrams, also in English, to show the production of salt, a video using local *sauniers*, salt workers, and products to buy. Entrance is free. Next door is **the Musée de Construction Navale**, Boat Building Museum, with many examples of boats built on the island, full size boat-builders' plans, part finished boats to show techniques, the tools used, and a self-explanatory video.

Just to the north of the town the **Bois de la Chaise** is an attractive wood of pine and oak criss-crossed by-roads with houses set amongst the trees. Three of the roads end at beaches. The largest and nearest to the town is the **Plage des Dames** with a pier for boat excursions across the bay to Pornic an hour away. Further on along the road towards l'Herbaudière is **Grand Viel** with its mile long (1.5km) beach **Anse de la Clère.**

Not far from the last village on the island, **l'Herbaudière,** is a shop selling the renowned *faience* from the pottery at **la Chapelle-des-Pots** (see the section on Saintes). You drive down a small hill into the busy fishing port packed with gaily painted boats unloading their catches. Adjacent is the marina with nearly 500 yachts and motor boats and all round are shops, restaurants and cafés giving this little village a lively atmosphere. You can take sea and fishing trips from the port.

SOUTH TO LES SABLES-D'OLONNE

La Barre-de-Monts is the inland half of this little conurbation and **Fromentine** on the sea is the port to the Ile d'Yeu. The town is both 'blue zone' and meter parking. It is a pleasant bright town with a nice shopping area and in the mile between the embarkation jetty and the bridge to Ile de Noirmoutier lies the town beach.

Beyond the bridge are sandy beaches facing the Atlantic and you can reach these through the Forêt Municipal using the town plan from the Tourist Office. The most northerly road by the municipal campsite should be avoided, since it is close to the local sewage plant. The next south reaches the beach and the third is flanked at a suitable distance by two naturist beaches.

Two miles (3km) inland is the **Daviaud Ecomusée for the Breton-Vendeen Marsh** where you can see life as it was at the end of the nineteenth century. It is based in a traditional house, *bourrine*, low standing with one room where the entire family lived. There are also salt marshes and an observatory to view birds

The attractive, rocky and small **Ile d'Yeu** 10 miles (17km) from St-Jean-de-Monts is only an hour and ten minutes away from its main port of Fromentine. In the summer boats run also from St-Gilles-Croix-de-Vie. The island is 6 x 2½ miles (10 by 4km) and its only town, village really, is **Port-Joinville**. Marshal Pétain, Head of State during the war and under the Germans, was exiled here where he died and was buried. While he lived in the Citadel from 1945 to 1951 his wife stayed at the Hôtel des Voyagers.

Explore the Ile d'Yeu

To see are the little **Musée Historial, Société Eel d'Yeu** for the breeding of eels, the **Grand Phare**, lighthouse, the **Dolmen de la Planche à Puare** in the north-west of the island, and the southern **Côte Sauvage** with the pretty little harbour of **Port de la Meule** sheltering in a cove in its midst. There are walks to be had either detailed in the Tourist Office brochure, or just by exploring on your own.

Notre-Dame-de-Monts is a smaller, quieter and less brash version of its big sister, St-Jean-de-Monts, to the south. The main part of the town is about 880yd (800m) inland, where you will find the Tourist Office, the Mairie and the church. The shops carry on down

the Avenue de la Mer to the Boulevard de l'Océan, an attractive promenade in front of the hotels.

Unusual happenings

There is a full summer offering of events both during the day and at night. In fact to keep a lighter touch on things than one might expect, they run both wheelbarrow races and an International Open for the... Frisbee.

If you prefer to walk through the pine forests and across the marshes, the Tourist Office will provide leaflets of waymarked walks from 7 miles (11km) to 14 miles (22km) long. To the east, 2½ miles (4km) away is a water tower, with a lift to the panoramic room. A little to the north of Notre-Dame on the main road is the well advertised Vannerie and Poterie (see the special section on interesting shops).

Between Notre-Dame and St-Jean turn off the main road to the **Pont d'Yeu**. Not of course a real bridge to the Ile d'Yeu, but rocks that stretch nearly 2 miles (3km) out to sea at low spring tides, to the delight of shell-fish gatherers.

St-Jean-de-Monts is the big resort on this coast. Here the **Plage des Demoiselles** with its surprisingly fine sand, seems to go on for ever. Between the hotels and apartment blocks and the sea the wide dual carriageway forms a magnificent esplanade. Many of the streets running down to the front are full of shops, cafés, restaurants and piano bars,

Above: Plage des Demoiselles, St-Jean-de-Monts

Right: Shopping in St-Jean-de-Monts

Below: Tourist Train, St-Jean-de-Monts

Devilish pact

Tradition has it the devil made a pact with St Martin, who wanted to convert the inhabitants of the Ile d'Yeu. He would build a road to the isle in one night before the cock crowed if St Martin would let him claim the soul of the first Christian who crossed over. Thinking to give himself more time, the devil made the cock drunk, but this had the opposite effect, and unable to sleep the cock crowed in the middle of the night; thus the road was never finished.

which also face the sea along the esplanade.

At night this lively holiday town doesn't stop, in fact it starts again with its bars and restaurants, casino, discos and nightclubs. The busy heart of the town is 1 mile (1.5km) inland with its indoor and outdoor markets and many shops around the church. A big and accommodating resort, it is ideal for a family seaside holiday. A popular attraction for children of all ages is the **Atlantic Toboggan** just to the south at **les Becs**. A series of exciting water slides culminating in beautiful blue swimming pools offer thrills and fun every day in season.

Next south on the main road is the small shopping centre of **St-Hilaire-de-Riez** with its markets on Thursday and Sunday. At Bois Juquaud 3 miles (5km) north of St-Hilaire, in a *bourrine* is **Le Bois Juquaud Ecomusée de la Vendée.** Inside, the farm buildings are set out as they would have been at the beginning of the last century, with the out-buildings, threshing floor and vegetable garden, restored and renovated. During July and August re-enactments of village activities take place here.

Sion-sur-l'Ocean itself is a small resort with a rocky foreshore, though within 100yd (90m) to the

north is the start of the 16 miles (25km) beach along the **Côte-des-Monts**. It is quieter than its big sisters to the north and south, with walks through the woods behind the sandy beach. On Tuesdays and Thursdays the market is held in the square.

To get to **St-Gilles-Croix-de-Vie** follow the Corniche Vendéenne. You cannot park along its entire length, so stop from time to time in one of the side streets. Stop to see **les Cinq Pineaux**, the five or six or seven rocks, count them as you might, just off shore as the tide rises.

All along the Corniche there are many little coves with sandy beaches, some of which fill at high tide. In another mile (1.5km), stop for the **Trou du Diable**, Devil's Hole. Here, as with the Puits d'Enfer on the Corniche to the south of Sables d'Olonne, you need the right state of the tide and a stiff westerly wind to get the best effects of the sea surging up through the rocks. The Corniche leads you into St-Gilles.

Two villages grew up on either side of the Vie Estuary, known collectively as St-Gilles-Croix-de-Vie with the northern side being Côte-Croix-de-Vie, after their church of Sainte Croix, and the southern side as Côte-Saint-Giles. Now they are two very busy and popular seaside resorts.

Côte-Saint-Croix is the commercial half of the two towns. Right by the railway station is the fishermen's co-operative and upstream is the modern marina, the Tourist Office and car park. Running parallel the main shopping street, Rue de Géneral de Gaulle, extends past the church in the Place Guy-Kergoustin (markets on Wednesdays and Saturdays), and on into the Quai de la République. One shop to look for is the direct sales outlet for the local fish canning factory, Gendreau, along the Quai de la République.

The church of Côte-Saint-Croix

This is dedicated to the fishing community, being hung with nets and buoys. The new altar table with symbols of the miracle of the loaves and fishes carved on the side is attractive, but what will strike you more is the elaborately carved pulpit, with its statues of the evangelists and prophets.

Between the ports and the shops is a maze of streets lined with delightful one-level, whitewashed fishermen's cottages, where you step from the bustle of commerce and cars to sudden tranquillity. In one of the cottages in Rue du Maroc is a tiny museum showing an interior from the 1920s.

From the fishing port you can take a ferry across the river to the **Dune de la Garenne** and the northern part of the huge **Côte-Saint-Gilles** beach.

There are fishing trips from the port and a little further down the estuary are two boat companies offering summer time passage to the Ile d'Yeu, an hour and a half away. You can expect to leave between 8.00 and 9.00 in the morning and be back in the early evening.

Côte-Saint-Gilles' main shopping streets are Rue Gautte and Rue Pasteur, with amusements, cafés and restaurants extending round the corner to Quai du Porte-Fidèle. In the corner of the two the market is held on Tuesdays, Thursdays and Sunday mornings. Quai du Port-Fidèle leads on towards the hotels and apartment blocks that back the beautiful Grande Plage, itself sitting between the Dune de la Garenne and the **Dunes du Jaunay**. For a day at the beach you can park behind the pedestrianised esplanade near the Dune de la Garenne, or the Avenue du Pont Neuf by the Dunes du Jaunay, though arrive early in the day to park nearer the beach.

Brétignolles-sur-Mer has a $2^{1}/_{2}$ mile (4km) rocky foreshore backed by a sandy strip under low cliffs, where the access is limited. However there is plenty of parking along the road. The village lies inland and has good shopping for its size, then to the south the sand starts again at the Plage des Dunes running about 2 miles (3km) to the mouth of the Auzance.

At **Brem-sur-Mer**, one of the four wine producing areas of the Vendée you will find the **Musée du Vin** at the Moulin de Bellevue on the Route de l'Ile d'Olonne where the museum is in a real wine *cave*. You can taste and buy the VDQS wine of the Fiefs Vendéennes.

The Bird Observatory and the Twin Standing Stones

Start at the bridge to La Chaume. At the first roundabout carry straight on up the Avenue de 8 Mai 1945 and follow the road towards the Dunes caravan site with its wide sandy beach and plenty of rocks with tidal pools.

Follow the way out and turn left at the next road to Champclou running through the edge of the Forêt d'Olonne, where you can glimpse the steep inland sides of the dunes through the trees. To visit the supervised sandy Plage de Sauveterre on the Atlantic-side of the Forêt take the little road to the left just before Champclou.

Go through Champclou and over the salt marshes to l'Ile d'Olonne then on for Olonne-sur-Mer. There are signs for the Observatoire des Oiseaux and within a short distance turn right. Just beyond the car park is an observatory, with nominal charges, telescopes already set up, and with some of the most interesting and easily observed bird life across the salt marches.

At Olonne-sur-Mer turn left on the D80 to the N160 and cross to the signed Pierre Levée Château and Pierres Jumeaux. The château was built in the style of the late 1700s though you can only visit the front court and gardens. Slightly further on the left are the Pierres Jumeaux, two megaliths standing under the trees beside the road. Drive onto the N160 again by les Sables-d'Olonne Golf Course and turn left for the return to Les Sables.

Observatoire d'Oiseaux de l'Ile d'Olonne

☎ 02 51 33 12 97.
Open: July to August daily 9.30am-noon, 3pm-7pm

Château de Pierre Levée

Some wine producers in the Fiefs Vendéens

All are open every day Monday to Saturday:

Gaël Crochet, La Gachère, 85470, Brem-sur-Mer.
☎ 02 51 90 50 92.

Marguerite Barbeau, 10 Rue de l'Océan, 85470, Brem-sur-Mer.
☎ 02 51 90 54 03.

Bernard Ferre, La Clementine, 85440, Talmont-Saint-Hilaire.
☎ 02 51 22 10 89.

Xavier Coirier, La Petite Groix, 85200, Pisotte.
☎ 02 51 69 40 98.

LES SABLES-D'OLONNE

Les Sables-d'Olonne known as the 'pearl of the ocean', is a large seaside town with its enormous beach, **le Remblai**, its 1$^1/_2$ miles (2km) long front lined with hotels, apartments, cafés and restaurants and at the western end the Casino with the Tourist Office and swimming pool.

Early in the evening you will find many of the sun and sea bathers collecting in the cafés for a refreshing drink. Behind the front are the shopping streets, sufficiently intimate and narrow to shade the sun in the heat of the day, the indoor market and the church of Notre Dame built in 1646 by Richelieu.

Behind this are the fishing port, a small commercial port and the marina. All are well used and you can idle a lot of time away watching the fishing boats come and go along the Chenal. You may of course prefer to do this from one of the very many cafés and restaurants lining the Quai Franqueville facing the quay.

If you like markets you will find five here: the covered market in the Rue des Halles open daily in the summer; the Marché de la Chaume, the suburb across the Chenal, on Tuesdays, Thursdays and Sundays; The Cours Dupont on Wednesdays and Saturdays; the Marché Arago, Boulevard Arago, daily; all open in the morning; and the main fish market on Quai Franqueville, in the mornings and late afternoons and on Sunday mornings in July and August.

Although most holidays in Les Sables will be of sun and sand, it has sufficient entertainment for duller days. Ferries run from the Quai Guine to the marina and to **la Chaume**, the old fishermens' district of small pantiled houses contrasting with the high rise blocks of Les Sables. The **Maison du Saulnier**, salt museum, Route de l'Aubraie is in the salt marshes to the north of La Chaume and the **Musée de la Mer**, Museum of the Sea, near the Tour Arundel in La Chaume. For brighter days and with views around the bay is the **Tour Arundel** itself, a former *donjon* built in the twelfth century by a Duke of Arundel who invaded and stayed for over 60 years. Boat trips go both to sea and up the river.

The southern suburb of les Sables-d'Olonne is La Rudelière, with its camp site, tennis courts, football stadium, horse riding, a lake sailing school, a second casino, **the Parc Zoologique de Tranchet** in the Rue du Tranchet and a supervised beach.

The Wells of Hell

Driving the road to Port Bourgenay along the corniche watch for the **Puits d'Enfer** – the Wells of Hell. Here the hard schist is splitting into deep trenches and in a strong westerly wind the sea powers up through the fractures to produce some spectacular effects. In calmer weather you can peer over the cliffs into a surprisingly clear sea.

SOUTH OF LES SABLES-D'OLONNE

At **Port-Bourgenay** park up behind the Tourist Office and Post Office and walk round the Village du Lac for the interesting buildings surrounding the small lake. In 1985 a marina was built and the holiday village has developed from it: much of the architecture is exciting, all of it interesting. From the roundabout take the road past the Abbey down to the marina. You can wander along the breakwaters, or take a walk along the cliffs westwards towards the cove of La Mine about 1.25km distant. Just beyond the hamlet of **St-Hubert**, to the east, is the long sand spit called **Havre-du-Payré** with its supervised beach **Plage du Veillon**.

On the road to **Talmont-Saint-Hilaire** is the curiously named village of **Querry-Pigeon**. Pick up the signs for the *Souffleur de Verre*, glass blower, and you will find Jean-Michel Gauthier's studio a few yards along a road on the right. Watch him at work and see his products around the walls of his old stone built workshop. Although he seems always to be busy, either Jean-Michel or his wife will gladly discuss glass blowing with you.

By the junction of the road from Bourgenay and the main Talmont-St-Hilaire les Sables-d'Olonne road is a **Motor Museum**. With over 100 motor cars dating from the late nineteenth century and with a further 200 other vehicles of all descriptions in running order held in reserve, as it were, this museum is absolutely not to be missed by any car enthusiast. It was founded in 1976 by the present owner's father, M. Giron Snr who had bought his first veteran car in 1939. Some of the cars included are a 1906 Renault, 1911 de Dion Bouton, 1925 Model T Ford, a Bugatti and a Chevrolet Impala.

Richard the Lion Heart's fortress

In Talmont itself, the feudal castle sits above the main square of the town and the Tourist Office. It was first built in the eleventh century by William the Bald and was made successively larger each century until the sixteenth.

In 1154, it came to Henry II of England as part of Eleanor of Aquitaine's dowry, and a few years later in 1189 Richard the Lion Heart made it his most important fortress in this part of his French possessions. A few years later the French won it back again. Today it is an interesting castle to see with its keep, bell-tower porch, chapel, the remains of the living quarters including an interesting fireplace, the spiral staircase, secret stairways and panoramic views of the Talmont area.

To the south of Talmont is **Jard-sur-Mer** a village of holiday homes and camp sites where the beach is both sandy and rocky, and just beyond Jard is **St-Vincent-sur-Jard**. Here one of France's most respected statesmen in the first 30 years of this century, Georges Clemenceau, ended his days in retirement and his house has been preserved as a museum. It is situated alone, by the beach of this quiet holiday village of *gîtes*. Out to sea is the Ile de Ré, and reaching round to the left is the 6 mile (10km) sandy beach backed by the **Forêt de Longeville**, best approached from the D105 signed Le Rocher.

Just inland from Jard at St-Hilaire-le-Forêt is CAIRN (the Centre Archéologique d'Initiation et Recherche sur le Néolithique). Within a radius of 2 miles (3km) there are many Neolithic remains – dolmens (passage graves) and menhirs (tall stones), giving CAIRN an opportunity to exploit the area. Its forte is to show neolithic techniques, for example flint knapping, weaving, growing ancient food plants and the like. An interesting museum aimed mainly at adults, shows Neolithic life and how the stones were erected.

Behind the Mairie in the Camp de César in **Avrillé** is the tallest menhir in the Vendée at 23ft (7m) and one of the tallest in France. There were three here when the site was a post relay station called Les Trois Piliers, the Three Pillars, but in 1825 when the Mairie was being built, two were destroyed.

Just north of la Tranche-sur-Mer is **la Terrière**, a pretty whitewashed village with fishermen's attractive one-level houses.

Son et lumière

Many legends surrounding menhirs involve water, and in late July and early August Avrillé puts on a son et lumière show around the 'miraculous' spring of St Gré. The show starts at 9 o'clock at the Roi des Menhirs, King of Menhirs, in the Camp de César and both the spectators and the actors set off with chinese lanterns along the country lane 1 mile (1.5km) to the Fontaine St Gré for the performance.

La Tranche-sur-Mer is a large and friendly resort. With some 8 miles (13km) of beaches and all the shops and restaurants a seaside holiday-maker could wish for, this is a real seaside town. Fun of every description abounds from the soft sand during the day to the soft music at night. The Tourist Office is in the main square, la Place de la Liberté, where the Tuesday and Saturday markets are held. In July and August another is on Wednesdays in the Grière car park.

The district around la Tranche has been inhabited for the last 7,000 years, though the town with its narrow picturesque streets dates from the sixteenth century when the locals began to earn their living from the salt marshes.

These days it is all tourism. Cycles can be hired, flights taken and microlights hired from the local aerodrome, sailboard hire and tuition on the beach, sea trips to the islands, fishing trips and all kinds of physical sports. For the less energetic, **Les Floralies**, an impressive park full of flowers, is open from Spring to Autumn and the Tourist Train will take you round the sights of both it and the town.

Walks at la Tranche-sur-Mer

Through the Forêt de Longeville, starting from the Floralies. One is 2 miles (3.5km) long to the Dune de Paris, a 85ft (26m) high local landmark, another to the village of la Terrière, and a third of 3 miles (4.5km) to the Creux du Navire Merchant, another landmark.

To reach the **Parc de Californie** take the old coast road signed to la Grière. Here in 10 green and flowery acres (4 hectares) are over 300 species of birds, with birds of prey that are allowed to fly free, though only during the summer season. Another mile (1.6km) on is the funfair at **Sweety Park**.

The most southerly of the Vendée seaside towns is **la Faute-sur-Mer,** a modern town with its long sandy beach – the southern section available for naturists – its family atmosphere, market on Thursdays and Sundays and a Casino. To the south the wooded **Pointe d'Arçay** shelters the estuary of the River Lay, ideal for observing migratory birds. At **l'Aiguillon-sur-Mer** on the opposite side of the estuary are two sea water lakes, one for swimming and one for the sailing school, and a miniature port.

OCEANÎLE

Just south of Noirmoutier-en-l'Ile

Newly opened aquatic entertainment complex of swimming pools with all the excitement of torrents, ocean waves, waterfalls, toboggans, eddy pools, paddling pools and more. Sunbathing terraces and a restaurant will complete the day.
☎ 02 51 35 91 35.
Open: mid-June to mid-September 10am-7pm.

THE CHÂTEAU

Noirmoutier-en-l'Ile

There are both permanent and temporary exhibitions in the Governor's *Logis* and in the *donjon* (keep).
☎ 02 51 39 10 42.
Open: mid-June to mid-September 10am-7pm.

SEALAND AQUARIUM

By the dock, Noirmoutier-en-l'Ile
☎ 02 51 39 08 11.
Open: every day February to mid-November 10am-noon, 2pm-7pm; summer all day. Visit it in the evening during July and August when it is less crowded.

LE DAVIAUD ECOMUSÉE DE LA VENDÉE

Two miles (3km) inland, near Fromentine.

Allow up to an hour for your visit.
☎ 02 51 68 57 03.
Open: February, March, April, October to mid-November: 2pm-6pm, summer months 10am-7pm. Sundays & afternoons only.

LE BOIS JUQUAUD ECOMUSÉE DE LA VENDÉE

3 miles (5km) north of St-Hilaire.

Open: February, March, April & October 2pm-6pm, May, June & September 10am-noon, 2pm-6pm,

July & August 10am-7pm, Sundays, afternoons only.

Le Potager Extraordinaire

La Mothe-Achard – Follow the signs from the main N60 La Roche-sur-Yon to les Sables-d'Olonne road.

Between July and October when the melon, squash and marrow crop is ready you can feast your eyes on over three hundred curiously shaped, spotted, carbuncled, and just outright odd varieties of these vegetables.

☎ 02 51 46 67 83.
Open: July to October, 10.30am-12.30pm, 2.30pm-7pm; closed Mondays in September

Tour Arundel

La Chaume

☎ 02 51 32 08 34.
Open: 9am-7pm, free of charge; if closed apply guardian next door.

Parc Zoologique de Tranchet

Les Sables d'Olonne

☎ 02 51 95 14 10.
Open: May-mid-September 9am-7pm, mid-February to April & mid-September to October 10am-noon, 2pm-6pm

Motor Museum

Near Bourgenay

☎ 02 51 22 05 81.
Open: every day, 1st April to 15 October 9.30am-noon, 2pm-6.30pm, 1st June to 31st August, 9.30am-7pm; October to March school holidays only.

Talmont-St-Hilaire Château

In July and August there are medieval entertainments in the castle such as archery tournaments, medieval crafts, guided visits and medieval games for children.

☎ 02 51 90 27 4.
Open: every day March and October 2pm-6pm, April to September 10am-1pm, 2pm-7pm.

Cairn

Inland from Jard at St-Hilaire-le-Forêt

Museum; a cinema room with English commentary; bicycles for hire for a waymarked tour of the Neolithic remains in the area. Thoroughly recommended if this is your interest.

☎ 02 51 33 38 38.
Open: April to June, September 3pm to 6pm, guided tours at 3.15pm, closed Saturdays. July and August 10am-1pm, 3pm-7pm, guided tour at 11am, demonstrations at 3.30pm and 6.30pm; closed Saturday and Sunday mornings

Castle at Talmont-St-Hilaire

INLAND VENDÉE

La Roche-sur-Yon hardly existed before 1804, when it was made a military base by Napoleon to help keep the reactionary Vendéens in order. Originally named after the Emperor himself, it took over as the departmental capital from Fontenay-le-Comte but it wasn't for another 20 years that its unique road pattern was laid out. The perimeter road is in the shape of a pentagon, the internal streets on a grid and right in the centre is the large Place Napoléon with a statue of the man himself. He sits on his horse, facing east and ready to ride again to his greatest victories in central Europe.

What's in a name?

La Roche-sur-Yon has had 6 name changes in the last 200 years:

It became the 'Chief Place' of the Vendée on the 5th of Prairial in year XII of the Revolutionary Calendar; that is 25th May 1804.

It then took these names:
Napoléon on 10th of Fructor year XII.

La Roche-sur-Yon in April 1814 at the First Restoration.

Napoléon again in April 1815 for the 100 Days.

Bourbon-Vendée from June 1815 at the Second Restoration.

Napoléon-Vendée in 1848 at the Second Republic, and finally...

La Roche-sur-Yon again on 27th September 1870 at the Third Republic.

The main shopping streets lead from the west side of Place Napoléon where you will find the Tourist Office by the Post Office in the Rue Georges Clemenceau, and the Municipal Theatre in its own *place* off the Rue Salvador Allende, with its classic façade and curious fountain.

The indoor market is south-east of the Place Napoléon in Rue des Halles and beyond that in the Place de la Vieille Horlorge is the old bell-tower on the site of the château. Opposite the Vieille Horlorge is the Maison des Métiers, dating from 1780, and nowadays used as a permanent exhibition of local craft products.

SOUTH OF LA ROCHE

Approaching from the north, west or the east the first sight of **Luçon** is the 262ft (80m) high cathedral spire as it comes above the horizon some 6 miles (10km) away. It is a small cathedral town of 10,000 inhabitants, just on the northern edge of the Marais Poitevin with its Tourist Office opposite the Post Office.

The Notre Dame dominates the small city and you will catch many

Horse breeding

In the south-west corner of the pentagon on Boulevard des Etats-Unis at la Roche-sur-Yon is the **Haras Royale**, one of the most important in France. The Haras is part of the National Stud of twenty-three covering the length and breadth of France, the *haras* at Saintes is also visited later in the guide.

The Haras had been founded in 1665, so France would cease being dependent on importing horses, and would have a resource of its own. Like many others, the *haras* here was constructed in the middle of the last century on an 11 acre (4.5 hectare), site to supply the needs of the cavalry. The director's house is in the middle and around about lie the four stables each holding twenty-two stallions, a smithy, a saddlery, and all the other needs of a large stud.

From March to July the stallions are made available to breeders to service their mares in the Vendée, Loire Atlantique and Deux-Sevres. Many of the horses are raced, or enter trotting races, and so successful are they, the Haras derives a considerable part of its income from the winnings.

In the reception house there are technical panels and a video presentation to give an introduction to the Haras. The guide takes you to see the equipment, buildings and horses, and describes the daily life including the bridle and smithy schools. The horses are exercised every day except Sundays.

glimpses of it as you walk about the streets. Luçon's historical claim to fame dates from 1608 when Richelieu was bishop here (1606-1623) from the age of 21. It is likely that when he was here and so close to La Rochelle, he grew to dislike the power of the Protestants in that city resulting twenty years later in the siege he laid at its walls.

Park in the Place Richelieu by the cathedral. It was built of the local mellow limestone in the Gothic style that we call Early English. Do not miss the oldest piece of furniture in the cathedral, found to the left of the choir: a pulpit charmingly painted with flowers and fruits and used by Richelieu himself when preaching. Behind the cathedral is the cloister occupying three sides of a square and Bishop's Palace, though you will need to go outside for the best façade.

Make your way along Rue du Président de Gaulle past the Tourist Office on the right, and just behind the Mairie, is the entrance to the **Jardin Dumaine**, a true gem in town gardens. Originally it was the garden of the town house that is now the Hôtel de Ville. In 1830 Pierre Dumaine planted the alley of yews you see immediately on entering the gardens and today they are alternated with palms and fuchsias. Just to the left is a small tower: surely this must be the most tasteful loo in all western France! A walk across to the left will bring you to the cascade and the fountain shooting up 20ft (6m) in a magnificent fan formation.

Press on further round the park to the Grande Pelouse for the topiary subjects. Fables, based on those of la Fontaine and known to every French child, form the basis of their

Above: Haras, la Roche-sur-Yon

Left: Jardin Dumaine, Luçon

design: a stork, a rearing horse, a donkey and cart, a horse and rider, all in bushes of different hues spread around and across a large lawn.

The network of small shop-lined streets welcomes you, particularly on the second and fourth Saturdays each month when big markets are held, though each week the covered market is on Wednesdays and Saturdays. Around the 15th August a 5-day market and exhibition is held in the Champ de Foire, with a 10-day fun-fair at the Place du Port.

TO THE NORTH OF LA ROCHE

The **Château de Bois Chevalier** lies north of Legé off the Rocheservière road, D753.

There has been a defended site here in the same family for the last 1,300 years, but it was only when Olivier de Bois Chevalier served his king, Louis XIV, well in the Wars of Religion that he was allowed to build a moated château. And on the wall inside is a copy of the letters patent granting the approval in 1655.

The château is on two main floors with the cellars and kitchen under. It is entirely symmetrical, both inside and out, with three rooms on either side of the central staircase. The stair is remarkable, being built of granite that 350 years of feet have

not worn. In one of the bedrooms is a boat-bed, reputedly the one slept in by Napoleon and Josephine on a visit! The tour is led by the present lady owner, part of that same family, and in French.

Lac d'Apremont has been formed by damming the River Vie at **Apremont** village. About 5 miles (8km) long it has pleasant beaches and picnic areas at both Maché, where you can hire boats and pedalos, and at Apremont itself. Within this little village is a large château and castle built on a rocky promontory overlooking the houses and the valley of the River Vie.

Much of the feudal castle remains, dating from medieval times. The entrance gate and most of the outer walls are over 600 years old while the two magnificent towers were built 350 years ago. The view from the platform on the south tower is along the valley and over the lake, and on a clear day the isle of Noirmoutier can be seen.

After the railway line from Aizenay to Challans was closed, the local communities resisted attempts to have the lines ripped up between **Commequiers** and Coëx $7^1/_2$ miles (12km) away. Now it is used for the **Velo-Rail** – a novel pedal driven rail vehicle. Each vehicle has saddles for two pedallers,

Exotic birds

The home to the **Ferme d'Elevage**, Breeding Farm, for ostriches, emus and rheas is **Eurotruche** at **Maché**. The start of the visit, with a handout in English, is a 17-minute video explaining the differences between these birds, how they are raised, and the ultimate aim of the farm.

Feathers are used in the couturier trade and when the birds are slaughtered for their meat, the skin is made into handbags, shoes and clothes. The tour is not guided and you follow a path between the large pens each holding a male bird and his wife and harem. The birds enjoy following you, treading so carefully you may believe them to have taken deportment classes. Then comes the mini-farm with ponies, donkeys, ducks, geese and even a pair of hares. There are descriptive panels in French and you return to the reception and shop. In the the Auberge 'La Logerie' meals of ostrich or rhea meat are served.

and seats between for three children. Jump in and off you set down the single track through attractive wooded countryside. What happens if you meet someone coming the other way? Well, if he is returning from Coëx, he has right of way; you lift your Velo-Rail off the tracks, and put it back on when he's past. Real fun rarely comes more energetically than this!

At the other end of the Velo-Rail is **Coëx** and the **Jardin des Olfacties**: a garden astride a pretty valley. Entrance is by the church in the heart of the village. You walk through a garden of sweet smelling flowers, then, to prepare you for the wood, past a waterfall and through the grotto. The sun slants through the tall straight trees around the flower-banked brook wending its way down the valley. The path goes into the Tropic House, and then you are out into the main garden for areas of herbs, medicinal plants, and plants taken for granted at home which, brought together here, add up to an experience not to be missed.

CHALLANS AND AROUND

Challans is a clean and pleasant town with its Tourist Office in Place d'Europe. On Thursdays in July and August the whole town goes back in time a hundred years and stages its Autrefois Challandais, where all the shop staffs and others dress in the style of the beginning of the twentieth century.

On the second Sunday in July and the first in August the village of **St-Christophe-du-Ligneron** holds its **Puces Ligneronnaises** Flea Markets. With over 150 stands they get up to 20,000 visitors and there is plenty of parking. Stallholders come from all over Europe including Britain, and on the July date, there is usually an extra attraction. It is all in aid of Cancer Research. Although much of the stuff at French flea markets is expensive rubbish, it is the atmosphere and the chance of finding a real bargain that makes the day interesting.

To the north of Challans on the D32 is the pretty little village of **La Garnache** with an interesting feudal castle, **le Château de la Garnache**. It was a wooden tower on a motte in the year 1000, and the mound of the motte can still be seen. The stone castle was begun shortly after this and added to for the next 500 years. The owners were the Seigneurs de la Garnache, who became so powerful that they also built the castle at Noirmoutier-en-l'Ile.

Then the castle at la Garnache came into the hands of the de Rohan family who were Protestants, and this ultimately led to its downfall during the wars of Religion, when it was put to siege and on its capture was ordered to be dismantled by Louis XIII. Of its eight original towers only two remain. One, circular, is sliced in half vertically, and the other is square with only its bottom half existing. However for a French feudal castle it has a lot to see, including models of the castle over the years.

There is more to this castle than a brief description can portray, and Marie d'Hueppe, the owner and a descendant of General Charette (see la Chabotterie), will be on hand to take you round with a guided tour in English.

Five miles (8km) north of Challans is the tiny village of

Chateauneuf. The mill is well-signed from most directions and you will receive a kindly welcome from Michel Vrignaud and his wife who own and run it. They produce animal feed here at the rate of 1cwt (50kg) an hour and while this is happening, you will be taken up to the top floor by Michel where he will proudly explain the working of his mill and give you a hand-out in English.

Built in 1703, it has been in the Vrignaud family for four generations, some of whose photos can be seen on the wall of the café. A few winters ago the mill's tree (the main sail axle) was replaced. The old one now lies with worn millstones in the picnic area, and pictures on the wall of the café tell the story of how the new 4 x 23ft (1.2 x 7m) long oak giant was made and placed at the top of the mill.

Another mile (1.5 km) leads to the village of Sallertaine built on an 'island' in the marsh and so called because the main source of income for the village was salt from the salt marshes. It has two enormous churches: the old one now being used as a local life museum.

Sixteen businesses and craftspeople have got together, with Sallertaine as the heart, to create a craft and tourist group. All the businesses in the village are included in this enterprise, and amongst them are a Dried Flower Barn; a Glass Blower workshop; Duck Products (food); Hand Painted Fabric shop; a Pastry and Bread shop; Pinta, of which more below; a Wooden Toys' workshop and a couple of miles (3km) away on the main road at the Quatre Moulins, a Weavers Workshop.

Sallertaine is in the middle of the Marais Breton and the best way of seeing it close to is by boat. Pinta whose base is here in the village do more than just hire canoes; they put on special canoe tours. There are breakfast tours starting at 5.30am to see the marsh at day-break, lunch tours, and evening tours including dinner, when you will see the marsh as the day fauna beds down, and when the night animals and birds come out.

A flour mill for 400 years

Near to Sallertaine is the **Moulin de Rairé**, and well signposted too from all directions. Its proud boast is that it is the only windmill in France to have been in continuous production since it was built around 1560. During that time it has had a number of owners, and now the present ones, the Burgaud family in their sixth generation, have been there since 1840. Somewhat larger than the mill at Chateauneuf, the system of operation is almost identical; however here you can compare modern milling in the building across the yard where flour for human consumption is ground.

Inland Vendée

HARAS ROYALE
la Roche-sur-Yon

Entry is through the Porte d'Honneur, leaving your car outside.
☎ 02 51 46 14 47.
Guided visits in July and August, not Sundays 10.30am-noon, 2pm-6pm,
September and October guided visit at 3pm Monday to Thursday

THE CHÂTEAU DE BOIS CHEVALIER
3 miles (5km) north of Legé off the Rocheservière road D753.
☎ 02 40 26 62 18.
Open: 1st April to 1st November 10am-noon, 2pm-5.50pm

EUROTRUCHE
On the D948, between Aizenay and Challans you will see the sign for the
Eurotruche.
☎ 02 51 55 72 88.
Open: Easter to end of June weekends only 2pm-6pm, July and August every day
10am-7pm

APREMONT, CHÂTEAU
☎ 02 51 55 27 18.
Open: June-August 10.30am-6.30pm, other months 2pm-6pm

VELO-RAIL, THE RAILWAY PEDALO
Commequiers

Booking for two, three or four hours is advisable in the peak of the season.
☎ 02 51 54 79 99.
Open: April to mid-June Wednesdays and weekends 2pm-7pm, mid-June to end
August 10am-9pm every day, first two weeks September 2pm-7pm every day

JARDIN DES OLFACTIES
Coëx

Includes the Théatre des Parfums is where you can sample smells and buy
them too.
☎ 02 51 54 61 18. Open: June, July and August 10am-8pm

CHÂTEAU DE LA GARNACHE
To the north of Challans on the
D32. As you enter the town from
Challans, pull into the castle car
park on the left and cross the
road to the entrance.
☎ 02 51 35 03 05.
Open: Saturday and Sunday 2pm
to 6pm, evening light show each
Wednesday in July and August
from 9pm.

Jardin des Olfacties, Coëx

THE NORTH VENDÉE

To the west along the N137 is Montaigu, at the junction of the River Maine and one of its minor tributaries. On Thursdays a very large countryman's market sells an amazing variety of goods. The main visitor points for the town are the Tourist Office at the end of the pedestrianised rue Georges Clemenceau. Just round the corner in the floral Place de l'Hôtel de Ville, are remains of the town walls built along the cliffs formed by the two rivers and the museum in the Pavillion des Nourrices built in 1640.

Fort de l'An Mil, Puy du Fou

North-east along the D753 is **Tiffauges**. When Gilles de Rais, said to be the original 'Blue Beard', married Catherine de Thouars, she brought with her a number of lordships including Tiffauges, part of the fortune he dissipated before he took up black magic and alchemy. (See Machecoul above where he was called Gilles de Retz).

Tiffauges Château has 18 towers looking over a 7 acre (3 hectare) lake. Here today, you can see aspects of the middle ages brought to life with knights fighting and medieval war machines, with audience participation, shooting their missiles up to 492ft (150m). Unique in Europe is an alchemist's laboratory in the form that Gilles de Rais may have used as well as other spectacles.

THE PUY DU FOU AND THE VENDÉEN WARS

The final tragic episodes of the Vendeen Wars in 1796 occurred at the **Logis de La Chabotterie**, halfway between La Roche-sur-Yon and Montaigu. The charismatic leader of the Royalist troops, Charette, was resting here wounded when he was surprised by Revolutionary soldiers and captured. He was led away to Nantes, tried and sentenced to death six days later, where he is reputed to have taken command of the firing squad by saying to them: 'Take good aim men. Aim here,' and holding his hand to his heart, he said 'It is here a brave man should be shot.'

A day that can involve such drama should be well prepared. First and most important is to book your seats for the most spectacular event of all: **the Cinéscénie du Puy**

du Fou at any Tourist Office some days in advance. It is also worthwhile booking for the Vendéen dinner in the Relais de la Poste.

To make a really good day, start at the Logis de la Chabotterie at 10am as they open. You will be able to spend an hour or two there, having lunch at the Auberge right by La Chabotterie. In the afternoon you can spend some time at the **Ecomusée de la Vendée** in the **Château du Puy du Fou**, but allocate most time to the **Grand Parc**, the theme park. Then in the late evening it is on to the Puy du Fou.

In the introduction to this book you will find the short background that is needed for this day and you are recommended to read it. Being a civil war within a civil war, the French are not at all proud of this episode in their history, though now they are making some amends by opening La Chabotterie and elsewhere, and by putting on such events as the Cinéscénie to publicise it.

The visit to La Chabotterie is not accompanied. Furnished rooms of the *logis* are dramatised for the time of the wars with original furniture, clothes and arms. A 10-minute film on the Vendéen leader, Charette is shown and the history of the architecture of the Vendéen Logis (fortified farms) is displayed with some 20 models of other Logis in the department. Dramatisation of the Vendéen wars and the capture of Charette using dioramas and models, with spectacular lighting and sound effects can also be seen. Traditional dancing and singing groups perform outside and an enchanting walled garden planted for the end of the eighteenth century will delight gardeners.

Leave **Les Herbiers** by the N160 towards Cholet following the signs to the Puy du Fou 9 miles (15km) away and in $1^3/_4$ miles (3km) you are climbing the flank of the northern end of the **Collines Vendéenes**, the Vendeen Hills. At the top is the **Mont des Alouettes** commanding a view, so it is said, from the towers of Nantes to the spires of Luçon. Here there are two windmills, a chapel, and large parking and picnic area and a café-restaurant.

Windmill warning

The hills are almost all above 650ft (200m) above sea level, with the Alouettes at 738ft (225m). There were once eight mills on this hill, and in common with most others during the Vendéen Wars 200 years ago, by varying the position of the sails, they were used as signalling towers to warn of the presence of government troops. Follow the signs to the Puy du Fou.

'I am the living memory of this evening. I walk through the centuries, from family to family... I sing the song of all the Maupilliers...'. So says the story teller as he starts an hour and a half of one of the world's most spectacular Son et Lumière extravaganzas. But before you reach this most exciting highpoint of your day, try to arrive at the Château du Puy du Fou not later than 1.30pm.

Some years ago the Association du Puy du Fou (see below), made an unsuccessful film called Vente de Galerne, The North-West Wind. The story line called for an eighteenth century village, and the one that is now at the heart of the Grand Parc was built. Because the village, produced from original materials, looked very much as if it really had been there for over two hundred years, it sparked the idea of a historical and ecological theme park. Within the park there are many attractions and events happening all day and a number occurring at special times.

The most interesting continuous events include: The Arboretum of France, showing most of the plants, shrubs and trees native to or now established here; the Eighteenth Century Village with all its workshops, like the artist, wood turner and wood carver, smithy, calligrapher, stone mason and clog maker. Musicians play in the village hall with its authentic beams, and a tightrope walker performs; the Grand Carillon of bells rings every 15 minutes, and figures operate every 30.

The exciting and dramatic panorama of le Chemin Creux des Guerres de Vendée, Vendeen Wars Way, is continuously open. At the Lake and the Aquatic Organs, you can operate a set of nine fountains to play with the music coming across the water, or if you prefer, to your own pattern. The Fort de l'An Mil, Fort of the year 1000, shows life and buildings at that time, and the Medieval Town is safe inside its walls and portcullises with houses and shops where you can buy many of the goods produced, like dried flowers, herbs and stained glass.

There are a number of timed events and you are advised to arrive at between 15 and 30 minutes before the scheduled start-time. All could be considered trailers for the main event of the evening: Fête de la Chevalerie: an exciting and humorous performance mostly carried out on horseback: a knight's tournament, Cossack style riding, dressage, and to keep it all going, a Fool and his sidekicks.

Théâtre d'Eau: a water, laser and projection show that will have you marvelling at its ingenuity. Le Grand Spectacle de Fauconnerie: here, falcons, large owls, eagles and vultures swoop within a few feet of the spectator's heads, large birds are released from a tethered balloon 328ft (100m) above your head, and all are controlled by their handlers walking through the audience.

The Legend of St Philibert at the Fort de l'An Mil, a truly spectacular event with Viking ships, miracles, laughter, fighting and reconciliation. There is a Children's Theatre and other events, like tightrope walking and juggling to be seen.

The partly destroyed, and never repaired, Château du Puy du Fou is the backdrop to Cinéscénie, the exciting interpretation of the history of the Vendée. In front of the château is a lake some 220yd (200m) wide and 440yd (400m) long, then between you, the spectators, and the lake is the 98ft (30m) deep stage where much of the action takes place. Nevertheless the director has used the whole area to set his play: the château, the lake, its wide banks, the woods and of course the stage in front of you.

The two parts of the Château are each run on an entirely different basis. The Grand Parc is a limited company with full time staff. The Cinéscénie on the other hand is an association of 2,000 local people from the 15 villages around formed to enact scenes from the history of the Vendée. All the performers are amateurs and drawn from many trades and professions. Whole families are completely involved.

One such, the Chatrys, has two brothers, who are stewards with Air France, the wife of one, a doctor, and their two children,

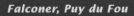

Falconer, Puy du Fou

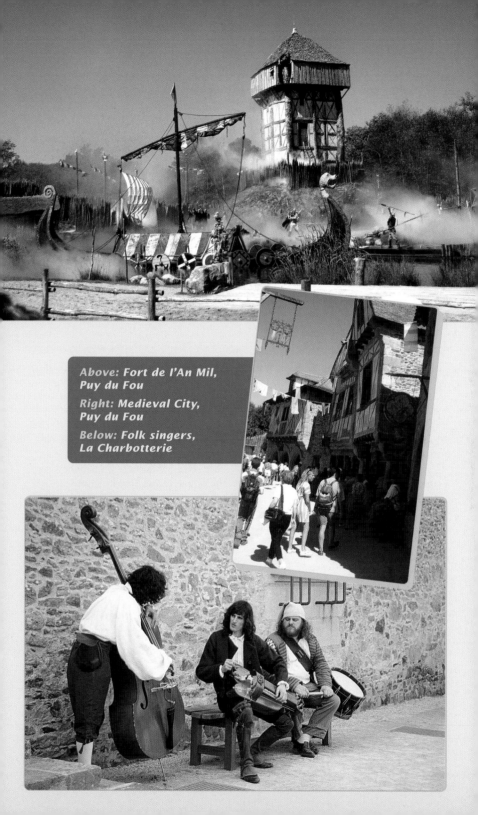

Above: *Fort de l'An Mil, Puy du Fou*

Right: *Medieval City, Puy du Fou*

Below: *Folk singers, La Charbotterie*

Synopsis of Son et Lumière

The story is set around Jacques Maupillier, Peasant of the Vendée. It tells of the Maupillier family whose eldest son in the great tradition of the Vendée is always nicknamed Jacques. It is 1916 and the story teller is spending an evening with the Maupillier family. Little Jacques is not yet able to see history in perspective and lets his imagination feed on the stories: Jacques l'Epourail with the pilgrims; Jacques Cornévache and the welcoming of Francis I to Puy du Fou; Jacques the Guardsman at le Puy du Fou; and Jacques the Conscript in the First World War.

Woven between the four Jacques is the daily life of the Vendéen peasant, his happy times and his triumphs, his sad times and his losses; the wedding, the dances of the *brioche*. Dramatic music, spectacular lighting, actors and horses apparently walking on water; tinted fountains; the château in happy times, the château burning; fireworks, lasers; giant image projection: it is all there and brought together in the grand finale staged around the Ballet of the Elves for a last extravaganza of light, water and fire.

who find time on twenty-six occasions in the year to take part in Cinéscénie. Each person is enthusiastically committed to the idea of the Puyfolais. In addition there has to be a small full time administrative staff to handle this £50 million business.

In the first year, 1978, they expected to play to a total audience of 14,000. In fact 83,000 people came along. Now, the 700 actors with 4,000 costumes, and 200 back-up staff are playing to 350,000 people every year, almost capacity. At the same time an even greater number of people are visiting the Grand Parc. The Puy du Fou is the third most popular attraction in France with only Mont St Michel in Brittany and the Palace of Versailles above them.

REMINDERS OF WAR

If La Chabotterie and Puy du Fou

have excited your interest, you may care to see some other sites of the Vendéen Wars.

In 1993 it was decided to build a modern memorial to the inhabitants of Grand-Luc and Petit-Luc who were massacred by the terror troops of the Convention (the governing body of the Revolution) on February 28th 1794. The **Mémorial de Vendée** at Les Lucs-sur-Boulogne, is in the form of a Way through buildings and a park setting with a description in English and has no charge for entry. The route takes you along Modern Memorial, called the Alley of History up to the 1867 chapel on a spur above the river and back through the park along the banks of the Boulogne. The chapel was erected in memory of the 564 inhabitants of Petit-Luc, and each of their names together with their ages is inscribed in marble.

Just outside the town limits on the road to La Roche-sur-Yon is a roundabout of concrete steles and bells forming the Monument Vendée 93. The town church has a stained glass window commemorating the victims of 1794.

Le Refuge de Grasla is 5 miles (8km) west of la Chabotterie in the Forêt de Grasla off the D7. The dispirited remnants of the Vendéen army retreated here in1793 to the depths of the forest where they had built a small village. Here you can see a forge, a charcoal maker's fire, the chapel, and events portrayed on video.

Places to Visit

North Vendée

TIFFAUGES CHÂTEAU

☎ 02 51 65 70 51
Open: March, April, May & September, Monday, Tuesday, Thursday, Friday 10am-noon, 2pm- 6pm, Saturday Sunday 2pm-7pm; June as above including Wednesdays; July and August every day 11am-7pm.

CINÉSCÉNIE

The performances are only on Friday and Saturday of each week from the last week in May to the beginning of September and if you need to, book the English language head sets, since the commentary and spoken parts are in French. (☎ 02 51 64 11 11, www.puydufou.com) The performances start at 10pm or 10.30pm, depending on the month, and it is advisable to take warm clothing.

LA CHABOTTERIE

Each summer Saturday evening there are musical events.
☎ 02 51 42 81 00.
Open: September to June, Monday to Saturday 9.30am-6pm, Sundays 10am-7pm; July and August 10am-7pm everyday.

GRAND PARC
Château du Puy du Fou

Fast-moving day out, with plenty of places to eat, from formal meals to fast food. Each person receives a brochure of the attractions in the park together with a timetable.
Open: May, Saturdays and Sundays 10am-7pm, June to mid-September, daily 10am-7pm.

MÉMORIAL DE VENDÉE

Les Lucs-sur-Boulogne, 5 miles (8km) south-west of la Chabotterie
☎ 02 51 42 81 00.
Open: September to June, Monday to Saturday 9.30am-6pm, Sundays 10am-7pm; July and August 10am-7pm everyday.

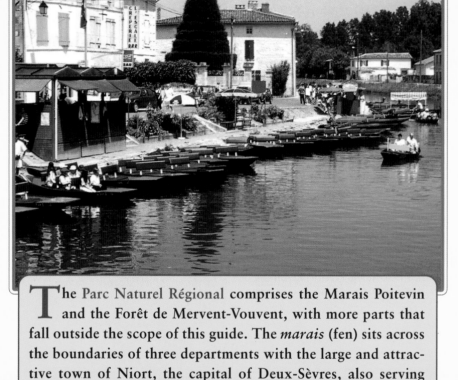

The Parc Naturel Régional comprises the Marais Poitevin and the Forêt de Mervent-Vouvent, with more parts that fall outside the scope of this guide. The *marais* (fen) sits across the boundaries of three departments with the large and attractive town of Niort, the capital of Deux-Sèvres, also serving as the capital of the Park. However for the best information you will need to go to the little town of Coulon for la Venise Verte, Green Venice, and to Marans for le Marais Désseché, the Dry Fen.

Just a short distance from Niort the River Sèvre divides into a network of waterways ultimately flowing into Aiguillon Bay, and the Poitevin marshland was formed from the deposits washed down by the river as it flowed to the sea. The open water areas silted up over many hundreds of years between the many islands that are today the sites of the towns and villages.

The land has been reclaimed for agriculture, first by monks, then the king, Henry IV, who brought in the Dutch, and finally Napoléon finished the job. The first inhabitants were the Colliberts who had the misfortune to be massacred by the Normans and were followed by les Huttiers who lived in *huttes*, huts, built with reeds. Tradition had it that ownership of a *hutte* was confirmed by building it in twenty-four hours with smoke rising at daybreak.

The **Marais Poitevin** falls into the two parts previously mentioned: the eastern and nearest to Niort is called **la Venise Verte** and the rest is called **le Marais Desséché**. The east is full of small and large waterways, sometimes through fields sometimes overhung with willows filtering the light to a pale green. This is indeed la Venise Verte. The traditional boats are the *yoles*, with pointed ends for fishing and getting about, and the *plattes* with square ends used to bring in the harvests and move the cattle.

In the middle, where it has been dry for many hundreds of years, there are fields of maize, sunflowers, linseed, barley and wheat, criss-crossed with hedges of bushes and tall trees along the drainage ditches. Then beyond Marans is the newest part of the fen which can still become flooded between December and May. The same crops are divided up by the many drainage ditches, with very few hedges and hardly a tree to be seen.

To the north and still within the Parc is the town of Fontenay-le-Comte and the Forêt de Mervent-Vouvent. To the east of the Forêt is the wine district of Pissot, a VDQS area and part of the Fiefs de la Vendée. To the south-east of Niort are a number of attractions: Melle with its Mines of the Frankish Kings; the Maison de l'Ane du Poitou (the Poitou Donkey Sanctuary) and the Zoorama Européen, a zoo with examples of nearly all the European animals on view. (See page 64).

NIORT AND AROUND

Niort is the capital of the Marais Poitevin Regional Park. It has a good shopping with two department stores, a number of multiples, very many independent shops and boasts a number of superb restaurants.

The Taverne de Maître Kanter, on the north side of the Place de Brêche can be singled out as a French café in the old tradition, in both appearance and menu, famous for its sea food, its eight kinds of *choucroute* and its home-smoked salmon. However, there are plenty more places to eat, notably in the area around the *Taverne de Maître Kanter* and also near the Donjon.

Local entertainment

From the 24th June to the 10th September the major buildings in Niort are floodlit, and at Christmas the shopping streets have spectacular lights. Each Thursday from the end of June to the end of September, the town provides free entertainment: dancing, plays, exhibitions, both on the streets and in a number of the public buildings. Then in the Place de la Brêche on the third Thursday of every month is a large market.

In the first century AD the Romans founded *Novio Rito* – New Ford – on the west bank in a meander of the River Sèvre. The town was protected on three sides by the river, with only a small neck of land to wall off. However, being low lying it was subject to flooding and, after the break-up of the Roman Empire, was persistently attacked by both the Vikings and the Franks.

The population moved across the river to the other hillier side so they could watch for raiders coming up the river. The two hills of St André, to the north, and Nôtre Dame with the small valley between were the original area of the medieval town. Later, when Eleanor of Aquitaine married Henry II of England bringing Niort as part of her dowry, Henry decided to fortify the town, and between him and his son Richard the Lion Heart they built the *donjon*, a wall round both it and the then existing castle.

A further wall $1^3/_4$ miles (2.75km) long round the town was put up reaching as far as the Place de la Brêche. The people settled the hill of St André, as you can see from the narrow twisting streets, while the nobility stayed on Nôtre Dame.

The export of wine and the import of salt brought Niort to commercial importance during the middle ages, and the inhabitants drew pride and profits from their fairs and markets, their Market Hall being amongst the most attractive in the French kingdom. This huge hall had been built in 1206 and occupied the whole of the present Rue Victor Hugo, from the shoe shop at the northern end to the brick and stone building at the other.

Niort's most famous son, actually in this case a daughter, is Françoise d'Aubigny, who after becoming a mistress of Louis XIV was made the Marquise de Maintenon, a delightful pun on the word *maintenant*: now, of this moment. Later, like so many towns in the area, Niort's prosperity was based on trade with Canada until it became British in 1763. But from the 1300s skilled craftsmen made the main industry the production of chamois leather for gloves from sheepskins softened with fish oil.

Angelica

The whole region round Niort is famous for its angelica and the city is known as the *berceau*, or cradle, of angelica. You can buy it as the Liqueur d'Angélique, and as sweets or for cooking: it deliciously flavours trout, omelettes, brioche, ice creams and rhubarb. There are a number of specialist angelica shops or, if you can become part of a party of seven or more (with the help of the Tourist Office) you can take a guided tour of le Logis d'Hércule, Maison de la Peste (the House for curing the Plague) with its 'quasi-divine remedy' of green angelica. The *Logis* is found round the corner from the Hôtel du Pilori. You are served the medieval remedies at a large round table by the *Maître* dressed in costume while you absorb the charm of the sixteenth century building and the angelica – the herb of angels. The half-hour tour takes place on weekdays in July and August and a resumé is available in English.

The Tourist Office is in the Rue Perochon near Place de la Brêche, the very large square in the middle of the city where you are almost always certain of a parking spot. Alternatively you can park near the Donjon on an island in the river. The diverse shopping area lies between the two.

The Donjon is an immense building looking exactly as you might expect a medieval castle to look, built as twin towers later joined by curtain walls forming a courtyard. In the fifteenth century the walls were raised in height, floors and then the roof were added, taking on the appearance it has today. Nevertheless it was an extremely strong castle with walls $11\frac{1}{2}$ft (3.5m) thick with few and small windows, entry being by a doorway high in the wall with access by a wooden ladder. These days though, it is easier! The two towers are 89 and 75ft (27 and 23m) high.

Inside is a museum in four main sections with the commentary cards in French and Braille: an art gallery with changing exhibits; a Poitevein interior, similar to the many other museums of its type, though displayed with more realism; a collection of head dresses, *coifs* (lace and embroidered head dresses). Each village had a shape, each family had its own style, and each female member had her own decoration. Then in the basement the Archaeological Museum: the finds from Niort and Deux-Sèvres include a gold necklace from the beginning of the Iron Age, a Celtic bronze cart wheel from Coulon in the Venise Verte, Roman items and coins and counters from the middle ages.

Continued on page 60...

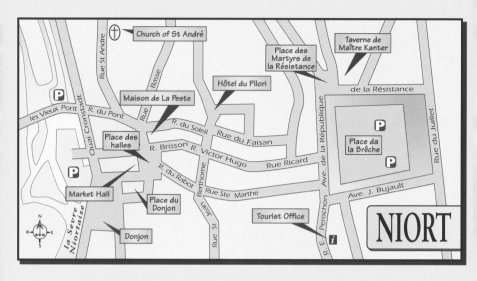

Map of NIORT, showing: Church of St André, Rue St André, Rue Basse, Place des Martyrs de la Résistance, Taverne de Maître Kanter, de la Résistance, Maison de La Peste, Hôtel du Pilori, les Vieux Pont, R. du Pont, Quai Cronstadt, Place des halles, R. du Soleil, Rue du Faisan, Ave. de la République, Rue du Juillet, P, Place da la Brêche, R. Brisson, R. Victor Hugo, Rue Ricard, R. du Rabot, Berthome, Rue Ste Marthe, P, Market Hall, Place du Donjon, la Sèvre Niortaise, Rue St Jean, Donjon, Tourist Office, R. E. Perochon, Ave. J. Bujault

The Dragons, Niort

Above: **Feudal Castle, Niort**

Right: **Ruralies Museum**

Below: **Aurochs, Zoorama Européen**

Musée de la Machine

Before you leave the Donjon make sure you go to the roof of the northern tower, for the viewing table and a view of the town and the tiles of St André area. Below the Donjon by the river is a market at the week-ends of *bouquinistes* stalls, book sellers, in the Coulée Verte running along and across the islands in the river. Beyond the parking are the *Vieux Ponts*, and the restored Tannery area below the St André hill.

Next to the Donjon is the Market Hall, built in 1869 of cast iron and recently re-glazed with heat reflecting glass. It is open every day except Monday, and the outdoor markets are on Thursday and Saturday. Walk into Rue Victor Hugo, where the huge original Market Hall was sited in the Middle ages, and on the left up Rue Berthome is the Pilori, sited on the old town pillory and the original Hôtel de Ville. These days this delightful building both inside and out, is used for temporary exhibitions of high quality.

The streets to the right of Rue Victor Hugo are pedestrianised and lead to the Hôtel de Ville, worth seeing, and the **Musées des Beaux Arts and Histoire Naturel**. And straight on from Rue Victor Hugo will bring you to the Place de la Brêche.

SOUTH-EAST
OF NIORT

If you are travelling from Paris to Bordeaux on the A10 Autoroute, the service area at Les Ruralies between junctions 32 and 33 makes a welcome and different halt. From Niort though, you can approach it through the town of Vouillé on the D948 about 4 miles (6km) to the east.

From Vouillé it is well signed – head for the **Musée de la Machine Agricole**. In the extensive motorway service area is a complex of shops, restaurants, a hotel and exhibits.

The Museum is a must for farmers and those with any interest in the development of agriculture. It traces agriculture over the last 200 years with examples of machinery, in several cases following the development of a particular machine. The tractor section will excite the most urban of visitors showing many examples from the earliest in 1913 to the 1950s. To add a bit of fun, set the 'Heath Robinson' machine going and if this doesn't make you chuckle, make the 1648 seed sorter sort some seed. Outside is a garden showing many forms of useful plant, an apiary and goats, sheep and pigs.

MELLE AND
THE SILVER MINES

Sited at the junction of two main roads, the D950 and the D948, is **Melle** renowned for centuries as a 'mule town' where the famous Baudet du Poitou was once bred (see the section 'Pôles-Nature') though the name comes from the Latin *Metallum*, Metal Town. Melle is a treasure. It is a treasure of a town today for visitors, and for Charlemagne and his successors it was their money tree. Here is a delightful old town situated on a hill with all the things a small town should have: narrow, winding streets, attractive old houses, wide open spaces in the middle, a market hall and a bandstand.

And as if that wasn't enough, it has the **Mines d'Argent des Rois Francs**, the Silver Mines of the

Frankish Kings, and a splendid 2 mile (3km) arboretum walk. The Tourist office is just outside the heart of the town by one of the three classified churches. You can park near the Market Hall (markets on Thursdays) and the English speaking assistant will arrange your visit to the Silver Mines and see you have the leaflet for the arboretum walk: *'Chemin de la Découverte'*.

You can drive to the Silver Mines, though it is perhaps better to leave your car where it is and walk the 440yd (400m) or so through the town. The visit is conducted in French with a good English résumé available.

At the start of a visit the guide will actually mint a coin – in lead not silver – to show the old method. The most important coin made was the *denier* (the d in our old £sd), worth 36lb (16kg) of oat bread or 24lb (11kg) of wheat bread. Then follows

a seven-minute film, in English on request, and a tour of the small museum. On the way to the mine, you stop at the Carolingien garden with over 100 herbs used for medicine, cooking and dyeing as they would have been at the time of Charlemagne (768-814).

Up to 12 miles (20km) of tunnels have been discovered, although the visit will only cover 383 yd (350m). Your visit is accompanied by the soundtrack of the specially written music and effects 'Glittering Silver'. You see how access was made down narrow shafts and the guide shows you the other minerals present including limonite, an oxide of iron, used by the Gaulish warriors to paint their bodies, with the Romans giving them the name *Pictones* 'the painted people', from which came the word Poitiers.

Continued on page 64...

Walk in the Arboretum
Chemin de la Découverte

When you leave the mine complex walk down away from the entrance area to the small lane and turn left to the Lavoir de Loubeau. Cross over the pretty humpbacked bridge and turn right to join the old railway line now converted to the arboretum walk, the **'Chemin de la Découverte'** (free entry at all times). The next 2 miles (3.2km) are a pleasure indeed. Over 1,000 trees and shrubs from all over the world have been collected and planted here. Flowering plants, large trees, small trees, trees that are decorative in the summer, and those that are decorative in the winter. Every season supplies its pleasures.

The path follows an old railway and crosses a number of roads leading back into Melle, so your walk can be as long or as short as you wish, and at no point is it more than half a mile (0.8km) from the middle of town. Where you cross the Niort road, is a picnic spot and toilets, and just down the hill one of Melle's three ancient churches, St Hilaire (see below). A little further on is the Bosquet d'Ecorses (Bark Copse). The walk routes you back into the north of the town.

History of the mines

The mines were lost between the tenth and the nineteenth century, and only found because quarrying the very hard Jurassic limestone for roads began on the site in 1822. The mines had been worked from at least the fifth century AD to the tenth when a number of real and imagined problems arose.

The Vikings were raiding the Atlantic coast and coming to Melle to rob the silver and take the skilled foundry masters into captivity, while the prodigious use of wood for smelting eventually led to local deforestation. Additionally the superstitious nature of the people led them to stop mining after an earthquake at Maixent-l'Ecole, a few miles away, added to the impending arrival of the year 1000 when it was firmly believed the end of the world was at hand!

Through the Jurassic limestone, water percolated for millions of years, and seeking out weak spots produced geodes, oval shaped cavities measuring upwards from a few inches to a foot or so (10-30cm) in size and containing quartz. Into the geodes came the water carrying with it salts of lead, silver and many other metals. The greatest deposits were of lead, with silver less than one per cent of that. Lead was in great demand for making pipes, plates, roofing and stained glass windows. The silver in the galena (lead ore) was used for minting money, the king seeing he had the monopoly.

The Silver Mines, Melle

Left: Shopping in Niort

Below: Hill of St André, Niort

Outside the caves are areas where archaeologists have carried out experiments in mining, and a set of life-size model furnaces show the method of extracting the metals and how the silver was separated from the lead. It was from the 'magical' separation that metal workers earned the reputation of being alchemists.

The town boasts three ancient churches dating from the twelfth century in 'Norman' style. In St Hilaire, where services are still held, you can listen to sacred music from around the world through a 'juke box' and buy it too. St Pierre holds artistic exhibitions throughout the summer months, and at St Savinien there are similar exhibitions and a music festival in May and June. You can easily allow yourself most of a day to see this delightful little town.

For the Maison de l'Ane du Poitou (the Poitou Donkey Sanctuary) see the feature Pôles-Nature. However when you leave the sanctuary make sure you go in the direction of **Chizé** where 3½ miles (5.5km) beyond you come to the **Zoorama Européen.**

The Zoorama is the only zoo in the area to be run by a department. It contains nearly all the animals to be found in Europe from ducks and hens, through otters and beavers to bison, aurochs and wild boars: just some of the 600 or so animals in the 62 acre (25 hectare) forest-park.

You can walk round, not an onerous task, or take a horse drawn *calèche*. Many animals appear to be happy here. But even though the zoo authorities have tried to give each as near a natural habitat as it can within the confines of the park,

it is obvious many are bored, and some disturbed. The main benefits it must be said, are that we have a chance to see the beautiful rare animals of Europe, and that a number are being saved from extinction.

Even more important, they have stocks of the aurochs, an ancestor of domestic cattle, and the tarpan, the same wild horse seen on the cave drawings of 25,000 years ago. Both these animals had become extinct by the early part of this century, and some careful back breeding has produced a new breeding stock of both species. Leave the Zoorama for **Beauvoir-sur-Niort.**

Restored windmill

Just before Beauvoir-sur-Niort is the tiny hamlet of **Rimbault** the home of a restored windmill that had been worked for many hundreds of years until it finally fell into disuse in 1928. A local society was formed, les Amis du Moulin de Rimbault, and restoration began in 1975. By 1976 the roof had been repaired, the sails were replaced in 1981 and it actually began to grind corn again in 1989.

During the third week of July on three nights a *Son et Lumière* presentation is given by the *Amis* and the local people with the sponsorship of the department. There are views across the undulating countryside towards St Jean d'Angely from this normally breezy place.

VENISE VERT

To take a drive around the **Venise Verte** leave Niort on the D8 for Magné and then make your way to the middle of **Coulon**.

This was a pretty town... once. As if trying to guard them from the outside world, the attractive houses have thrown a ring around the market square and the church. They failed though, and the world has taken over with a vengeance. Many of the houses have been turned into poor quality, expensively priced tourist traps, selling cards, local wines, and tacky gifts. To one side is the Tourist Office; and looking across at it all, and undoubtedly shrugging its shoulders in true Gallic fashion is the pretty pantiled church.

From this square you can take the tourist train (the *Pilabou*) on an hour and a quarter trip of 12 miles (20km) or hire a bike at the café. One of the shops contains an Aquarium of river fish and is worth a visit. No little tiddlers, but giant carp 3ft (90cm) long and weighing 35 lb (16 kgm), pike up to $4\frac{1}{2}$ft (1.30m) and the biggest of all, a silure at 4ft 9in (1.44m).

Boat hire

Walk down to the river, le Port, to the *embarcaderie* where there are a number of firms offering boats for hire at high prices. You can be accompanied by a French-speaking guide who will also paddle your boat; or for about 20 per cent less you can paddle your own.

Along the riverside is la Libellule, the Dragonfly, a shop selling the tastes of the Marais: Rabbit Paté; Cochet d'Or, an aperitif made from dandelions – *pissenlit* in French; Torteau Fromage, a cheese bread; angelica sticks and the alcoholic drink, Angelique de Niort. Many will find this shop is more attractive than those around the church.

Further along is **La Maison des Marais Mouillés** (The Wet Marsh House) the Ecomusée in the old Maison de la Coûtume, a sort of Customs House that collected taxes from cargo boats using the Sèvre Niortaise River. There is an exhibition, well worth seeing, of 'Then and Now' photographs of the Marais and Niort. The inside of a Marachaine house is also displayed and the Maraiscope, a cross between a *son et lumière* show on a model of the Marais and a spectacle of slide images recounting the development of the area.

Leave Coulon by the D1 towards **Sansais** and in $2\frac{1}{2}$ miles (4km) take the D102 right, to **Le Vanneau** and **Arçais**. On the way you pass the **Parc Zoologique de la Venise Verte**, a little zoo specializing in the flora and fauna of the area as well as a number of dwarf animals, always popular with children. It occupies one of the limestone promontories reaching into the fens and goes down to an old cliff formed by the sea in times past.

Arçais is a pleasant little town with the Hôtel du Marais in its middle. Turn left into the little square with the church and the Post Office. At end of a narrow passageway marked with the green *Artisanat*, sign is a courtyard.

Above: La Venise Verte
Below: Le Pilabou, Coulon
Opposite Page: By the river, Coulon

Here you will find a charming barn holding the Artisanat Arçais with a selection of good quality gifts made by local craftsmen and craftswomen, including the local dandelion aperitif 'Cochet d'Or'. Go down the Rue du Grand Port to the attractive riverside frontage with off-road parking. There is a restored crane, boats for hire, but without the brashness of Coulon, and a modern river-trip cruiser leaves from here.

The pretty drive to **Damvix** has little houses and bungalows on the opposite bank, many with their own fishing *yoles* moored below them. Park over the bridge facing the river. The boats are prettier here in their gay colours against the green of the water and of the willows on the opposite bank. The hotel, the Moderne, a *crêperie,* a restaurant and cycle hire are in town and, half a mile out, horse riding.

Be sure to walk round the charming old streets. Down the Rue de la Poste and on either side there are little *impasses* each with its own character, one with a barn, the next with roses. Turn back towards the middle of the village and just by number 9, Rue de la Poste are two old, two roomed traditional Marais cottages. Turn into the Rue de l'Industrie on the left by the church past the triangular barn with a dwelling behind it, then two more regularly shaped barns, but can you see which one is vertical?

Flower-decked village

Follow the road through to **Vix** and as you enter the village there are two private gardens on the left, each a riot of flowers. Flowers tumbling out of trees, down from windows, and the topiary even has bespectacled figures sitting on seats. Unlike most villages to the south in Charente-Maritime who boast of their twelfth- and thirteenth-century churches, this village boasts its modern 1974 church whose bell tower is of reinforced concrete.

Leave the village and reach the main D938 where there are views over the central part of the Marais. Turn right towards Fontenay-le-Comte and then take the Niort road.

FONTENAY-LE-COMTE

Some of the previous owners of the delightful 'L' shaped **Château de Terre-Neuve** on the outskirts of **Fontenay-le-Comte**, were keen alchemists like so many of their aristocratic contemporaries. Among the large collection of pestles and mortars are two attributed to Benvenuto Cellini, who lived in Florence from his birth in 1500 to his death in 1571. Above the porch

door is a short poem by Nicholas Rapin, the original owner, asking the winds to let neither fever nor plague, nor envies nor quarrels enter the house.

Tour of the Château

In the sitting room that dates from the eighteenth century, the beautiful fireplace is called the Alchemist's, from the esoteric carvings and the Latin quotation from Seneca, 'From our birth we are dying each day'. The chair, a *dormeuse*, was used as a sitting-up bed by ladies who did not wish to disturb their highly dressed hair.

Through the Francis I door carved with his 'F' and Salamander and into the dining room where there is an eighteenth-century sedan chair, nicknamed a *vinaigrette*, because the occupant was usually shaken about. This room is magnificent with its ceiling of carved stones, of more alchemist's insignia and a beautiful Sèvres swan-necked chocolate service on display. The fireplace is supported by two large griffins and has carvings of the Fairy Mélusine, a local fable (see Vouvant).

A later owner, Octave de Rochebrune, was a trained artist and had the hobby of engraving pictures. Using his copper plates, a limited number of prints are made which are on sale. In 1866 many of the best features of this house: fire places, ceilings and so on were expropriated from the château of Coulognes-les-Royaux at Coulognes-sur-l'Autize about $15\frac{1}{2}$ miles (25km) away!

To go into Fontenay leave the

Château along its drive of chestnuts and turn right down the hill. The Tour Rivalland, the strange octagonal tower looking over the rooftops, is 82ft (25m) high and was built in 1880 by a rich freemason, G. Rivalland. He took his freemasonry rather seriously and did not want the church spire to dominate the skyline. For all that, what is really different is that the top four floors are of concrete poured into shuttering: a skill that was not developed elsewhere in Europe for another ten years; and the metal crown is not a lantern, but a complicated form of lightning conductor!

Famous residents of Fontenay

François I, king of France from 1515-1547, was one of France's most famous kings, patron of the arts and scholarship in the Renaissance and a humanist. He called Fontenay 'a fountain and source of great minds', a title that was later transferred to the town fountain itself. This was the time of the Renaissance, and Fontenay attracted a number of people who were questioning the teachings that had gone before.

Among them was François Rabelais, (1494-1553) best known for his satire on the church and the aristocracy, 'Gargantua and Pantagruel'. He was followed at the end of the century by Nicholas Rapin, a poet who had the Château de Terre-Neuve built by his friend and architect Jean Morisson, and by another friend François Viète, the mathematician. Although these people were still closely involved with the Church this was the beginning of the Humanist Movement we know today.

Fontenay was originally at a ford over the River Vendée near the present Pont Neuf, the bridge on the main road through the middle of the town. In 1471 when the town was thriving from the cloth and leather trades, it was given its charter.

The Tourist Office is the Pavilion d'Octroi, a little octagonal lodge built in 1845 in the area of the then developing port and served as one of ten toll houses at entries to the town. You can find it at the junction of the Rue du Port and the Quai Poey-d'Avant just down stream from the Pont Neuf with plenty of parking space in the vicinity.

The best way to explore the town is to walk. Leave the Tourist Office along the arcade of shops that runs to the Rue de la République, the main shopping street, with the Palladian style fronts opposite and turn uphill to cross the Pont Neuf. Carry on to the Market Square (markets Wednesdays and Saturdays) where the **Musée Vendéen** and Notre Dame church can be visited.

Go past the church and left and right into Rue Pierre Brissot where there are a number of town houses 300 and 400 years old. The Hôtel de Grimouard has the solid wooden door and the Latin inscription stating the house was restored in 1741. At the bottom, turn left up the Impasse Mouillebert to the old feudal castle, now in ruins and still of stupendous size, its dry moats forming attractive walks in the Parc Baron. To the right of the Impasse is the Rue Goupilleau, where at

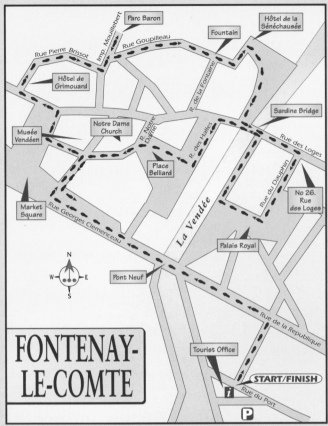

FONTENAY-LE-COMTE

du Dauphin, second right past the Sardine Bridge, will bring you to the Palais Royal, and in its present condition it would be hard to find a building looking less like a Palais Royal. Doorways and windows are filled with breeze blocks, and behind the antique and rusting wrought iron gates are weeds 4-5ft (1.5m) high, not to mention the modern 'improvements'. What a sad period for such a good building.

number 6 in the reign of Henry III, bandits made coats of mail.

Straight on brings you to the Fountain that gives the town its name. An unsuccessful attempt was made to repair it at the end of the fifteenth century and what we see today dates from1542. Down the hill and round the corner is the Hôtel de La Sénéchausée (1590), the replacement for the cold and draughty feudal castle. Go to the river and on to the Sardine Bridge, so called from the fish market for the fishing boats coming up the river to sell their catch.

There are a number of old houses in the pedestrianised Rue des Loges opposite, number 26, with its iron balconies and numbers 85 and 94 further on are worth a visit. The Rue

Go beside along the river on the small Quai Colin, and back over the Sardine Bridge. Turn into the Rue des Halles with the giant terracotta flower pots decorated by local school children. Across the road is the Place Belliard, also called the Places aux Porches where large markets were held both in the streets and under the arches until the end of the nineteenth century.

Leave the Place at its top end passing the gate of the Hôtel de Rivaudeau. In Rue Notre Dame on the left is the beautifully carved Hôtel de La Perate and the former Palais de Justice now a primary school. Return to your car through the Market Square.

Above: Château de Terre Neuve, Fontenay-le-Comte
Below: Sardine Bridge, Fontenay-le-Comte

THE FORÊT DE MERVENT-VOUVANT

This forest is an area in total contrast to the Marais to the south. Here is a high zone of granite with deep steep-sided valleys, four of them dammed to produce long winding lakes from the waters of the River Vendée and its tributaries.

About 2 miles (3km) on the D938 towards Châtaigneraie, is **Pisotte**, a wine area of the Fiefs Vendéens, and in about another mile (2km) take the small un-numbered road on the right marked Barrage de Mervent. The road is one-way for about 3 miles (5km) and passes the lowest dam where you can park for views over it. Follow the road for Mervent, and at the D116 you can divert towards St-Michel-le-Cloucq for a small zoo, the **Parc Animalier de Pagnolle.**

Mervent is a very small village with a lot of surprises and built on the top of a hill in a meander of the main reservoir. Here is a small Tourist Office, where you can get leaflets for many way-marked walks through the forest.

Surprise clock

A small 1,000-year old church, across the square from the Tourist Office in Mervent, has a treat inside: a weight driven clock. There it sits with its tiny face, masses of well oiled machinery and the two weights to one side. Then inside are the handles used to wind it up every 7 days. It chimes at the half and the hour.

The village square is the site of the entrance to the *Hôtel de Ville* and the public gardens. At the balustrade 100ft (30m) or so above the reservoir, is a nice view of the lake with its little island, the fishermen in boats, and the forest all round. Drive to the bottom of the hill again to the lakeside and pick up the signs to the **Château de la Citardière,** now a *crêperie* in a most attractive red granite building set on three

sides of a square and surrounded by wide moats.

Over the moat bridge are exhibitions of paintings, sculpture and tiles through a number of unrestored rooms; though you may find the wonderful old fireplaces, the windows overlooking the moat and musket firing holes equally interesting. The *partagère,* cooking stove, on show is similar to the one seen in the Château Terre-Neuve at Fontenay. During July and August, the *crêperie* puts on a series of musical evenings from jazz to operetta.

At the hamlet of les Quillères turn left for **Vouvant.** This village rightly claims to be 'one of France's most beautiful'. It has two squares: the first recently re-paved outside the church, and the second by the Fairy Mélusine's Tower.

The north door of the church has some of the best-preserved carving to be seen in this region. Among the extravagant scenes of animals and flowers, on the left-hand side, Delila is shown cutting Samson's hair and on the right, he is seen wrestling with the lion. Walk round too and see the carved window pediments. The inside, in contrast, is very plain.

There are one or two nice shops near the church, and three better than usual cafés. In the middle ages the town was fortified with an encircling wall and towers; all that is left is a section of the walls and postern gate, above the lake, seen best down the pretty roads past the pharmacy.

Further sections surround Fairy Mélusine's Tower, the last remains of the feudal castle, and the Tourist Office with more leaflets for forest walks and guided tours of Vouvant. The Café du Centre will give you the

The legend of the Fairy Mélusine

Mélusine is a local fairy credited with many magical powers, not least the instant building of the castle at Lusignan, where she is in bas-relief, as well as the castles at Pouzauges, Tiffauges, Mervent, Vouvant, and Parthenay! The legend goes that she had killed her father, and was condemned to turn into a fairy-serpent every Saturday. By the time Vouvant comes into the story, she had married Raimondin, Count of Poitou, who soon became consumed with jealousy at her regular disappearances.

To find out the truth, one Saturday he broke down the door to her room with a single stroke of his sword. Utterly amazed, he found her transformed to a fairy-serpent washing and combing her long golden hair. So surprised was she that her secret had been discovered she immediately flew out through the window and took on her serpent form. She slithered three times round the town and Lusignan castle, and disappeared in thin air. The Lusignans, the family that built the feudal castle at Vouvant, claimed descent from Mélusine and Raimondin.

key to the tower to climb the 120 steps to the top.

Take the road to the back of the Tourist Office, D31, and after 880yd (800m) follow the signs for *miel*, honey, leading to **La Haute-Motte** about a mile (1.5km) away. Here you can see the interior of hives, honey extraction, a video, how the bees tell each other where to find the flowers and of course taste the many types of local flower honey that Yves de Rosanbo, the owner, collects in a 30 mile (48km) radius of Vouvant. On Thursdays M. de Rosanbo demonstrates the collection of honey from the hive outside the building, while spectators are inside and protected from the bees. On sale every day are beeswax candles, furniture polish and honey. Return to Fontenay along the D938.

MARAIS DÉSECHÉE

From most directions Marans church spire is visible across the fens. The almost transparent spire comes as somewhat of a surprise after so many solid ones. But this is what it is: a spire made of special tubular sections. Park up in Place Cognacq at the top of the main street of this busy little town and you will find the Tourist Office a few yards down. Here you should ask to be taken up to the panoramic viewing platform in the bell tower 118ft (36m) above the town. When the present church was built in 1902, the money ran out before the bell tower could be built. (See box on page 74).

Leave Marans taking the N137 for 6 miles (10km) north towards Chaillé-le-Marais, then 800 metres short of Chaillé turn off left along the D25 to Triaize. The first village is **Ste-Radegonde-des-Noyers** with its windmill and there is another in the next, **Puyravault**.

Lying along the low limestone ridge barely rising above the fens is **Champagne-les-Marais** with its ar-

A gift of thanks

Eight years later in 1910, a son of the town, Barthelémy Fabbro, left for fame and fortune in Paris at the age of 16, and in 1987 having made that fortune, decided to give Marans a gift. He chose the bell tower as being the most appropriate. The town welcomed the opportunity, and used as much home-grown talent as possible to design and build it. The tower is of the local pale limestone, and the spire was manufactured by a Marans ship mast firm in aluminium tube. In the viewing room are descriptive panels made by the technical school.

On Mr Fabbro's birthday, the 28th July 1988, the spire was to be raised by helicopter, but it was too windy and the attempt failed, then a few days later, the 49ft (15m) high three-quarter tonne construction was safely put in place by crane.

tisan pottery shop. The personable little square has everything important in French village life: the church, the post office, the *boulangerie* and the *marie* where you can get leaflets for two fen walks.

From Triaze to St-Michel-en-l'Herme you are in a land of low horizons and high skies. Everything is dominated by blue on fine days and by grey on cloudy ones. The *EDF* (French Electricity) has crisscrossed the entire fen with lines giving some interesting perspectives, though difficult to call picturesque.

It was as late as the dark ages that farmers came to reclaim the salt marsh for agriculture and the name of **St Michel-en-l'Herme** derives from Latin, *in eremo*, 'the deserted place'. Around a bend in the road, the farm of les Chaux is standing on a small hill above the flood plain.

The Tourist Office is in the town next to the seventh-century Benedictine Abbey, with a half hour accompanied visit. Should your taste be inclined another way, you may care to join in their *Grenouille* Party at the beginning of August

each year.

From St-Michel take the D 60 for **La Dive** about 5 miles (8km) away. Further inland the high spots of hard limestone have weathered into hills with gentle slopes; not so these outer hills that were the last to be islands in the Poitevin Bay. La Dive is almost surrounded by low cliffs, and some of the stone was

A hill of shells

The hill at les Chaux is all that remains of massive mounds of oyster shells, most of which were sold to a now defunct factory where they were pulverised as an additive to cattle feed. (There is a picture of the mounds and the factory in the exhibition at the Maison des Marais Mouillés at Coulon.) Call at the farm and they will show you the shells. Whether the mounds go back to pre-historic times or the Middle Ages has not been resolved.

Above: Reservoir, Mervent
Right: Tour Melusine, Vouvent
Below: Château de la Citardière

used to make the sea wall a short way further on. Park on the top for the view to the south of the bridge to the Ile de Ré and the harbour installations of La Rochelle.

Carry on to the coast road and turn left to the Pointe de l'Aiguillon. The sea wall is rather high here, but there are steps you can climb to see over the mud flats and the *bouchots* of mussels. Finally, past

the café is the Pointe with wide open views of the Bay of Aiguillon and the Ile de Ré bridge. The oyster and mussel boats come into the bay on the flood tide from the ports to the south for the day's catch.

Return the way you came to St-Michel-en-l'Herm and at the church take the minor road across the Marais to **St-Denis-du-Payré**. From the *Mairie* at St-Denis you can get a

Places to Visit

DONJON

Niort

☎ 05 49 77 16 74
Open: daily, except Tuesdays 9am-noon, 2pm-6pm, 5pm mid-September to early May.

MUSÉE D'HISTOIRE NATURELLE

Niort

Combined ticket for this and Donjon available.
☎ 05 49 77 16 74.
Open: daily, except Tuesdays, 9am-noon, 2pm-6pm, 5pm mid-September to early May

MUSÉE DE LA MACHINE AGRICOLE

Prahecq

☎ 05 49 75 68 27.
Open: daily 10am-6pm, 7pm in summer.

MINES D'ARGENT DES ROIS FRANCS

Melle

Allow up to two hours for your visit.
☎ 05 49 29 19 54.
www.melcom.fr/mines
Open: March to May, October to mid-November, weekends and holidays, 2.30pm-6.30pm, June to September, daily 10am-noon, 2.30pm-7.30pm.

ZOORAMA EUROPÉEN

Melle

A nice touch is that each visiting party is given a descriptive book in their own language showing every animal. Your visit here should be about three hours and there are plenty of places for a picnic.
☎ 05 49 77 17 17.
e-mail cenes@wanadoo.fr.
Open: February, March, October, November, 9am-noon, 2pm-6pm, April, May, June, 9am-7pm, July and August, 9am-8pm.

RIMBAULT WINDMILL

Beauvoir-sur-Niort

Allow half an hour for an accompanied visit and a quarter of an hour for an unaccompanied visit.
☎ 05 49 09 79 39.

leaflet showing an attractive walk of about 4 miles (6.4km) through the woods to the north of the town.

A mile (1.6km) further on towards Triaize is the **Réserve Naturelle Michel Brossélin** for an accompanied tour of about an hour. The site is managed by the Association de la Défense de l'Environment en Vendée, and the guides are all volunteers. The best time to see the birds is either at 10am or at the end of the day just before they close.

Return the way you came through Triaize and at Chaillé-les-Marais pick up the D25 again and go through a handful of sleepy little villages to the D938. Left on the main road is Fontenay and Niort, right Marans.

Niort & the Marais Poitevin

Guided Tour May to October, 2nd and 4th Sundays of month 3pm-7pm. Or by appointment.

LA MAISON DES MARAIS MOUILLÉS

Coulon

Allow an hour or even more for this worthwhile exhibition.
☎ 05 49 35 81 04. www.ville-coulon.fr, e-mail mmm@wanadoo.fr
Open: February to end November, Tuesday to Sunday, 10am-noon, 2pm-dusk, June and school holidays, daily as above and weekends to 8pm, July and August daily 10am-8pm.

CHÂTEAU DE TERRE-NEUVE

Fontenay le Comte

Tour conducted by English speaking guides and takes less than an hour.
☎ 02 51 69 99 41.
Open: May to September 9am-noon, 2pm-7pm.

MUSÉE VENDÉEN

Market Square, Fontenay le Comte

The museum was founded by a local artist in 1875 and is in the ancient Presbytery of the church. Interesting exhibits of Gallo-Roman glass, a model of the town in Renaissance times, and a collection of regional furniture.
☎ 02 51 69 31 31
Open: June to September Tuesday to Thursday 10am-noon, 2pm-6pm; Saturdays and Sundays and rest of year 2pm-6pm.

PARC ANIMALIER DE PAGNOLLE

Nr Mervent.

☎ 02 51 69 02 55.
Open: 15 March to 1st November 9am-nightfall

PARC DE PIERRE BRUNE

South of Vouvant, off the Mervent road.

Children's park of Pierre Brune in the heart of the forest. With its little train, bumper boats, mini go-karts, radio controlled boats, botanical garden, it is a delight for children of all ages.
☎ 02 51 00 20 18.
www.mervent-foret.com
Open: daily 1st April to 1st November 2pm-7pm, weekends 10am-7pm; June, July, August daily 10am-8pm.

This department has three major historic towns, two beautiful islands ringed with soft sandy beaches and one major seaside resort, and between them all, France at its most rural. Historically it has four distinct phases: the Roman occupation 2,000 years ago; the building of almost all the churches 1,000 years later; the wars with England and of Religion between 300 and 500 years ago; and the present.

In Saintes there are the Roman Arena, the Baths and the Arc de Germanicus to see. All over the countryside are churches in the style called Roman here, which we call Norman at home, and built in the eleventh and twelfth centuries. If this is your interest, you are in seventh heaven. At La Rochelle and at Rochefort, the Wars of Religion between the Catholics and Protestants supported by the English, were played out and what has been left behind is particularly beautiful.

The isles of Ré and Oléron and the Royan district fully represent the last 100 years with their beautiful sandy beaches, their salt and oyster industries, and the growing of *primeurs* – early vegetables; and should you want to find them, the relics of the last world war. No quality wine is produced here but what is grown are the grapes whose wine is eventually made into cognac and Pineau des Charentes, a delightful mixture of wine and cognac.

Treasures of the Saintonge

Saintonge is the old name for the district of Saintes, which was superseded after the Revolution by the name of the department. However we are all nostalgic, none more so than the Tourist Offices in the Saintes area. They have brought together a number of must-see châteaux, museums and buildings all of which are well maintained and well run, and consequently well worth visiting.

Should you have the misfortune to have a rainy day, then one of the museums should be your destination, but the châteaux will need to be seen on fine days, since you will probably want to stroll around their gardens.

The Tourist Board has selected a number of buildings of outstanding appearance and interest to be Les Trésors de Saintonge, the Treasures of the Saintonge District. The more important of them are described in this guide and are marked with a special T at the top of the box (See above).

 Do not miss.

 Try not to miss.

 Worth the journey.

No star: See only if you have time.

LA ROCHELLE

Here is a vibrant city with modern roads and industry around its charming historical heart. It is THE urban tourist area of the region and as such has much for both the business person and the holiday maker.

There are plenty of hotels in **La Rochelle**, a whole district of specially designed holiday flats and hundreds of restaurants. A thriving commercial port placed well away from one of the largest marinas on the French Atlantic coast, shops of all descriptions, two man-made sandy beaches and an atmosphere of its own that will captivate you from the moment you arrive.

Parking is very difficult and very restricted in the middle of the town. However, there are a number of free car parks within a short distance. Recommended is one in the Esplanade du Parc, about 440yd (400m) north of the Place Verdun, the town bus terminus. Alternatively follow the signs to the Minimes and the Port de Plaisance where there is almost unlimited parking. Catch the *Bus de Mer* into the Old Port, and you can come back up to 11.30pm in the summer.

What is now Charente department, took quickly and fervently to Protestantism at the time of the Reformation in the mid-1530s when John Calvin preached in the area. The Protestants in their zeal destroyed all the Catholic churches in the town – except the towers, which were used for navigation.

But in 1562 the Wars of Religion began and lasted until the end of the century when the French king, Henri IV, proclaimed his historic Edict of Nantes, giving many rights to Protestants and naming specific cities of security, including La Rochelle. The peace was not to last long. Eleven years later, a Royal army was at its gates putting it to siege but after six months the Royal forces had lost 20,000 men and the siege was raised. The city, whose prosperity was based on its maritime trade, became even more prosperous. Then under the excuse of religious uniformity Cardinal Richelieu, King Louis XIII's First Minister, started to reduce the political importance of Protestantism.

Meanwhile, the English, the French Protestants' most enthusiastic supporters, sent the Duke of Buckingham to take the Ile de Ré in 1624. Unfortunately for the Duke, the island had a courageous new governor, Toiras. He had already defeated the Protestants on the island and reinforced the Fort de la Pré and the main town of St-Martin. In fact today you can see his name crudely engraved into one of the paving stones in the church at St-Martin, as THOIRAS.

The English landed at Sablanceaux, at the island end of the present bridge, and laid siege immediately to the Fort de la Prée and St-Martin. The French King himself arrived with reinforcements outside La Rochelle, and despatched a part of them to relieve the garrisons on the Ile de Ré. The English were caught between two armies and soundly defeated. Toiras was appointed a Marshal of France.

Richelieu against the English

La Rochelle was under siege and a year later, in 1627, Richelieu was put in charge of the languishing attacks since the English were still giving assistance to the city by sea. To stop this he built an immense dyke across the entrance to the port. First he sank old ships filled with stones, then built the dyke on this base. However, the strength of the tides prevented the final closure, though the gap was sealed by floating ships, which stopped the English bringing relief. In the *Hôtel de Ville* you can see the dramatic picture by Henri Motte, of Richelieu on the dyke watching a sea battle and the same thing in waxworks in the Musée Grévin.

Leading the city against the besiegers was the mayor Jean Guiton, whose statue is outside the *Hôtel de Ville*. When he was appointed he is reputed to have said: 'I will be mayor. But see this dagger! Be sure I will plunge it into the breast of the first man who asks for surrender, and what's more I will plunge it into my own if I should propose the same...'. So saying he brought it down forcefully on the marble topped table which is still on view today in the *Hôtel de Ville* complete with its dagger mark.

The siege continued for another two years with the city reduced to a famine that cost 28,000 Protestant lives. The dead were piled high in the houses, and when the Royalists marched in, only 5,000 people were alive. At the surrender the delighted Catholics took over the city and started rebuilding their old churches. The king paid for the new cathedral to be built in an imposing style to impress on the Protestant population that Catholicism was here to stay.

Today, 350 years later, you can see what is left of the dyke: the red tower (called Tour Balise de Richelieu) off the Port de Plaisance indicates the deep-water channel, and at the place that was not closed off all those years ago, a spit of rocks still reaches out at low tide.

A WALK ROUND LA ROCHELLE

This fascinating walk round one of France's most interesting and historical sea-ports ensures you see all the interesting features, and still gives you time for relaxation and shopping.

Make your way to the **Vieux Port** (Old Port) and the **Tour de la Chaîne**. It was here the chain that allowed entry and exit to the port was controlled. Only those with peaceful intentions could enter, and only those who had paid their port dues could leave! The tower was built around 1325, and it was not until the seventeenth century that the battlements were removed. Inside is a museum with a model of the city at the time of Richelieu and an exhibition of paintings and sculpture.

Continued on page 84...

Go round the tower and up the steps to the Rue sur les Murs, Street along the Walls. When the desirable houses behind you were built, water lapped the wall 30ft (9m) below, and what a view they have.

At the end is the **Lantern Tower** used as a prison for British, Dutch and Spanish sailors (termed 'pirates' in the French handouts at the tower – such is our European chauvinism). These sailors, having little else to do, cut over 600 drawings on the walls of their prison including people, ships, buildings and even one locomotive.

You will find reference to *Les Quatre Sergents* too. After the defeat of Napoleon, and with the restoration of the Monarchy, some of the officers of the regiment sent to La Rochelle for garrison duties were zealous republicans opposed to the Monarchy. They were arrested and before going to Paris for execution, were held in the Lantern Tower where they contributed to the graffiti. The tower is 184ft (56m) high, the lantern being placed in the small tower on the north-western side. From the top you have clear views of the sea-roads and the islands.

At the crossroads walk down to the bridge in the Rue de la Monnaie, Mint Street. The little stream running through the park is all that is left of the original port of the city, replaced by Eleanor of Aquitaine's more central Vieux Port.

Turn back to Rue de St Jean du Perot, a street of many ethnic restaurants from Indian and Thai to a Steak Bar. The most important however, is Andre's, THE sea food restaurant whose proprietor also sells fresh fish from stalls on the pavement each morning. Walking on towards the Grosse Horloge is the Musée Grévin which shows the history of La Rochelle in a series of 16 waxwork tableaux – there is an English handout.

Go through the **Grosse Horlorge** into the Place Petits Blancs. During July and August only, the Grosse Horlorge is open for a view of the town, with an archaeological museum on the way up. On the corner of the Rue du Palais and Rue du Temple, the renaissance building shows its original windows to advantage. The statue here is to Eugene Fromentin, a local author.

Perfume bottles

Above the *Parfumerie* at 33 Rue du Temple is Anne and Jean Seris' pride and joy, an internationally known **Musée du Flacon à Parfum,** Museum of Perfume Bottles, truly a museum that is different yet fascinating. Jean will proudly show you the press reports and tell you that the museum featured on television and has a number of exhibits in the Louvre in Paris. A pleasant three-quarters of an hour may be spent viewing over 50 glass cases containing an amazing variety of metal, crystal, and glass creations (including Lalique), in every size.

As you go round this city make a point of looking up from time to time. There is yet more to be seen in the upper floors: for example the half-timbering appears to be disguised. To prevent the salt in the air rotting the timber, it has been covered with a thin screed of cement and then decorated with slates. Often too, you can see the gargoyles that threw the rain off the roof. What it was like to be in the street in a storm 200 years ago can only be imagined!

When the Dutch came here to help drain the marshes, they brought not only their knowledge of water management but their architecture that immediately appealed to the careful nature of the Rochelois. As in Holland, many of the houses are built narrow, the stairs slim in proportion, and with most space given to the rooms. Many a top floor has a gantry to get the furniture in through the windows.

Back to the Place Petits Blancs and cross straight into the Rue Chef de Ville to take the second turning on the right, Rue d'Escale, where the pavement is decorated with multicoloured pebbles. **Charente-Maritime** has had long-standing connections with Canada. There was a big trade in furs, a lightweight cargo, and to sail better the ships need to sit deeply in the water. Each ship carried ballast of St Lawrence River pebbles, then with no further use the careful Rochelois used them to pave their streets.

Further up the Rue Venette and in Rue Aufrédy is the Hôpital Mre D'Aufrédy. In 1202, it is said, the D'Aufrédy family sent their ships to the Near East intending to make a fortune. Year by year they waited for their return, until they slipped into penury, finally living with the poor. Then one day, eight years later the ships hove in sight. Rather than return to their life of luxury, the D'Aufrédys built their hospital as a refuge of comfort where the poor could get food and lodging in time of their distress. The present building is used by the Ministry of Defence for wounded veteran servicemen.

Turn right and past the *Hôpital* and left into Rue Perennial. On the first corner is the old Catholic church of St Barthélémy, one of the churches partly destroyed by the Protestants, and still with its tower for navigation.

Dr Venette

On the corner of Rue l'Abreuvoir and Rue Nicholas Venette is the house of Dr Venette who died in 1698 aged 65. He struggled to make a living as a doctor and even his first book on medicine didn't bring him any big reward. However when he wrote his book, *How a Wife can look after her Husband,* his fortune was made. The beautiful house was built on the proceeds of the first sex manual in Western Europe!

Cathedral of St Louis

At the next corner, in the Place de Verdun, is the cathedral of St Louis completed to its present state in 1648 though two towers were intended to finish the front. Inside is a magnificent and very large organ at the north end, and beautiful glass windows above the altar. The cathedral treasury contains religious objects from the La Rochelle area.

Above: Aquarium, La Rochelle

Left: Tower of the Grosse Horlorge, La Rochelle

On the right-hand side of the Place de Verdun you will find the Café de la Paix whose decor is still in that of the *Belle Epoque* of the turn of the century. Plan to stop here for refreshment: sit inside and absorb the charm and beauty of this splendid café. Go right from the café and right again to the end of Rue du Minage to the last remaining fountain the city used to provide clean fresh water, Fontaine du Pilori.

Daily market

Right yet again and you are in the Place du Marché and the market hall. It opens every morning in the year, spreading into the surrounding streets on Wednesdays and Saturdays. Four hundred years ago the Rochelois knew they needed a market hall. They could neither agree on its site nor on its style and it was another two hundred years before agreement was finally reached and the building begun. During this time wares were sold along the $5^{1}/_{2}$ miles, (9km) of arcades throughout the city. Opposite the market hall is the shortest street: Impasse Tout y Faut, Everything you Need!

Leave the market along Rue des Merciers, one of the main shopping streets – the others are Rue Saint-Yon and Rue du Palias, all running parallel to each other. Use the tiny Rue de Beurre to reach Rue Fleuriau and the Hôtel Fleuriau. The Hôtel Fleuriau, a building worth seeing in its own right and originally built by a prosperous shipowner, now contains the **Musée du Nouveau Monde,** the New World Museum, making the visit doubly worthwhile.

La Rochelle's connection with Louisiana, Quebec and the French West Indies, well-documented in carefully collected works of art, artifacts, photographs, paintings, maps and documents. Rooms are devoted to exploration, slavery, natives of the West Indies and of Canada and the United States. Items stress the Triangular Trade: manufactured goods to Africa, slaves to America, sugar, cotton and furs to Europe. Of continuous interest to North American visitors, the museum depicts French influence on the course of European expansion there.

Come back into the Rue Saint-Yon, and turn right towards the *Hôtel de Ville*. Before going in through the front of the *Hôtel de Ville*, go round to the Rue des Gentilshommes to the Porte des Gentilshommes, the entrance the aldermen used. To be made an alderman in the fifteenth and sixteenth centuries was an award not given lightly, so to enter this way was indeed a privilege: the front door was reserved for ordinary folk!

Above the door you will see the three-masted ship of La Rochelle with its sailor climbing the ratlines, and the architecture above appears to be out of square. However in the approach from the right, that made by the *Gentilshommes*, it returns to square. Monster faces appear on every second support and as a considerable concession in those days to the female sex, there are two women's faces!

Outside the main entrance is the statue to Jean Guiton the cobbles around the statue being set in the Protestant emblems of a star, six circles and a dove. There has been a *Hôtel de Ville* on this site since the twelfth century and the present one dates from around 1500 with the wall that faces the square built in the style of a fortification stressing the independence of the city.

Eccentric sundial

In the courtyard the sundial is said to be always 2 hours 50 minutes slow: one hour for summer time, one hour for central European time (the sun time at La Rochelle is the same as London) and fifty minutes for the *quart d'heure Charentaise*. The little door below the sundial leads to the tunnel system under the city, cut in the time of the middle ages.

At the top of the bell tower the original statue of Henry IV holding the Edict of Nantes was destroyed during the Revolution and was not replaced until the end of the nineteenth century. The main façade was erected in the years around 1600 by Henry IV and constructed in Italian style. On the ground floor is the columnar gallery and the initials of Henry and his wife Marie de Medici above it. Go under the arches to see the remarkable carved ceiling.

The figures higher up represent the four cardinal virtues: prudence, justice, power and temperance (she is pouring water not wine). A hundred years later the fifth figure of law was installed, and placed outside the mayor's office.

At the end of the Rue Hôtel de Ville is the narrow Petite Rue de Port leading onto the Quai Duperre. Turn towards the Hotel de la Tour de Neslé and cross to the Rue St Nicholas with its antique shops just behind. On Thursdays and Saturdays a Flea Market is held both here and in the adjacent Place de la Fourche, where the bric-a-brac stalls jostle with the lunch time crowds at the café tables.

From the end of the street you can cross to the Quai Gabut and make for the **Tour St Nicholas**. The Tourist Office is in the modern shop development of the Quartier du Gabut on the left.

The Tour was built at the eastern end of the town's fortifications and to complete the circle the chain was attached to it. Named for St Nicholas, the patron of seamen, it thus ensured the triple protection of the saint, the walls and the chain. Because of the marshy nature of the land in the fourteenth century it was built on a raft of oak, and only now is it beginning a slight tilt. It is 138ft (42m) high, with its four floors of strongly-built vaulted rooms, bedrooms, fireplaces and latrines, all combining to make a luxurious residence of the time.

Despite this, it is not an interesting building, most of the tour being in passages rather than rooms. It is steep up and steeper down, with the view over the water the only thing to see, rather duplicating that from the Lantern Tower.

You can only reach your car parking or the *Bus de Mer* by walking round the Vieux Port, and now is the time to take a well deserved rest at one of the many cafés on the Cours des Dames and maybe dinner later at André's.

OTHER SIGHTS IN LA ROCHELLE

Until September 2000 the beautiful **Aquarium** at Les Minimes is open until 11pm in July and August, giving an opportunity to come along when most of the crowds have gone home. There are thousands of specimens in the exhibits from the Atlantic Ocean, the Mediterranean Sea, the Tropics, the Caribbean and the Amazon Room. The most popular of all is the Shark Room with the sharks swimming round and round above you.

In January 2001, the whole thing removes to the Avant Port, just beyond the Tour St Nicholas in a bigger building costing £10,000,000. Two floors are devoted to the Aquarium, where the information panels are also in English, and a third for shops, restaurants and cafés.

The whole area beyond the new Aquarium is called la Ville en Bois, after the days when it really was a Town of Wood with warehouses and shacks for dockworkers. Now it is being rebuilt, and parts are still building sites.

The **Parc Charruyer** and the **Esplanade du Park** run a mile (1.5km) inland from the Rue de la Monnaie. Along the Allées du Mail, named after the game of pell-mell, is the **Casino**. In the **Port des Minimes**: **Musée Océanographic** has an accent on harvesting the sea, from whales to mussels, and shows animals and birds stuffed or as skeletons, and a pair of seals are fed at 4pm. There are two beaches: one here at les Minimes, the other by the Promenade de la Concurrence between the Allées du Mail and the Tour de la Lanterne.

The **Musée d'Orbigny-Bernon** has local and regional *faience* and Chinese porcelain on show, the **Musée des Beaux Arts** has works by Corot and William van Velde Jr, and the **Muséum d'Histoire Naturelle** includes a botanical garden.

AROUND LA ROCHELLE

TO THE NORTH

Esnandes lies at the junction of the rocks of La Rochelle and the marsh of the Marais Poitevin, a pretty little village of whitewashed cottages and narrow streets set out in a grid with car parks close by. Ever since the thirteenth century the inhabitants have been occupied in the raising of mussels on *bouchôts*, the poles you can see standing up out of the mud at low tide.

Mussel culture

It is said that in the fifteenth century an 'Irishman' called Walton was wrecked in the Anse d'Aiguillon and took up residence at Esnandes. In order to survive he caught and sold birds. To increase his chances of catching them he set up poles in the mud below the high tide mark and stretched his bird nets over them. Each day they were washed by the tide and soon he saw they were covered in little mussels who found the poles a suitable habitat. Thus began the *buchôt* system!

The church looks more like a fortress. Though founded as a church, it was fortified in the fourteenth & fifteenth centuries with a rectangle of walls over 13ft (4m) thick and battlements above. The bell tower also served as the *donjon* and there are good views from the parapets.

The **Maison de Mytiliculture** (mussels) traces the history of the Anse d'Aiguillon, the development of the *buchôts* system from the fifteenth century, and includes one enormous pole over 157ft (48m) long. The Tourist Office is close by.

Drive past the Museum and Tourist Office under the cliff, to the end of the road and turn up and take the zig (or is it the zag?) to your left to the viewing table with its clear and colourful representation of the scene across to La Pallice, Ile de Ré and the Pointe d'Aiguillon.

TO THE SOUTH

Châtelaillon-Plage is a small seaside town without the charm of a small town. In the Rue de Marché is the Market Hall, open every day, with a street market on Tuesdays and Fridays. To reach the sea it is necessary to go along rather poky streets to the front, the Boulevard de la Mer another narrow road with no parking. The beach however is 2 miles (3km) of fine sand stretching from Fort St Jean and the Casino in the north to the Port de Plaisance with its sailing school in the south.

TO THE EAST

Lying between St Jean-d'Angely and La Rochelle, the small town of **Surgères** has a large medieval castle with the church, the Mairie and the library in its grounds. Virtually all that remains is the long outer wall about 710yd (650m) round with some 20 towers, parts of the moat, Helen's Tower, named after Helène de Surgères, and the motte (an earthen mound). The curious renaissance gateway between the church and the Mairie carries the arms of the Maingots, the first owners, on one side, and the Rochefoucaulds, the last, on the other. The Mairie is in the 200-year old manor, with a beautiful staircase.

ILE DE RÉ – THE WHITE ISLAND

The main anchorages are on the northern coast with the beautiful sandy beaches almost all round. It was fortified by Vauban to guard against the British and Dutch and there is a lighthouse at the northwest point.

You need to pay the toll over the bridge to get on the island, 110 francs return for a car and 220 francs return for a car and caravan, though pedestrians and cyclists go free. Unquestionably, having to pay lends a certain exclusivity to the island, and many people believe it is a modest amount to pay for its beauty. The light is very special in May and June, and with less visitors in these months than later in the summer, an ideal time to holiday here.

Coming over the sweep of the 2 miles (3km) long, 97ft (30m) high bridge, the first village is **Rivedoux-Plage** with its north and south beaches of fine white sand. Here you meet the common and attractive style of painting the house shutters green and the wall footings with tar left over from boat painting. About $2^{1}/_{2}$ miles (4km) on the road to St-

Above: Street Boules,
Ile de Ré

Right: Hollyhocks, Ile de Ré

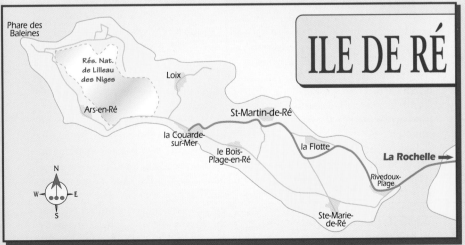

Phare des Baleines

Rés. Nat. de Lilleau des Niges

Loix

Ars-en-Ré

St-Martin-de-Ré

la Couarde-sur-Mer

le Bois-Plage-en-Ré

la Flotte

La Rochelle

Rivedoux-Plage

Ste-Marie-de-Ré

ILE DE RÉ

N
W — E
S

Cycling on the island

You can cycle along special cycle tracks, *Pistes Cyclables*, in complete safety since the whole island is criss-crossed with them and you can hire cycles in every town and village. This is the island of the cyclist, there being no hills (the highest point is only 65ft [20m]) and everywhere is accessible on two wheels.

Martin are the remains of **Fort de la Prée** on the right, where during the last war the Germans based a Big Bertha gun to protect the U-Boat pens at La Rochelle.

Some 820yd (750m) to the northwest are the remains of the Cistercian Abbey of **Les Châteliers**. Over the centuries the Ile de Ré has suffered with depredations both natural and man-made. In the tenth century the Vikings were raiding most coasts and Ré was no exception, where they pillaged and destroyed the economy. The island's feudal lord invited the Cistercian monks to establish this abbey and introduce their skills in producing both wine and salt, staples of the economy to this day.

Follow the road to **La Flotte** with its small boat haven and a medieval market under pantiled roofs, with a truly ancient tree in its midst. A short way further on is **St-Martin**, the chief town, and arguably the most beautiful in this region of France. It lies entirely within Vaubin's fortifications, today pierced to allow the modern road through.

Just to the east is the old citadel, today used as a prison for medium term offenders. The original citadel was destroyed by the Duke of Buckingham and later rebuilt by Vaubin for Louis XIV, the Sun King, whose effigy is above the main gate. In the nineteenth century and up to1938 it was used as a staging post for the prisoners intended for New Caledonia and Devil's Island, where parties were sent twice a year in batches of up to 600.

Final farewell

Opposite the Citadel's main gate is the original port used to take these prisoners out to their ships. As ships grew larger it was decided to march the prisoners into St-Martin, and in order to avoid contact, the local inhabitants were forbidden to venture out on those days. It was well known that to be condemned to New Caledonia or Devil's Island meant in effect a sentence of death, so the relatives of some prisoners used to hire a window in the town to catch a last glimpse of their loved ones.

The port here has two arms, so made as to almost create an island in the middle. Today the eastern arm is for fishermen, and the western for pleasure boats. Like most of the anchorages on the island it can only be reached through a lock at the top of the tide. There are many hotels and restaurants facing the port from both the town and the 'island', one of which, the Baleine Bleu on the 'island' has a first class restaurant and a bistro for faster meals.

Storm protection

That many of the buildings throughout the island are one floor only is very noticeable; in La Flotte are a number of houses with two floors, and now here in St-Martin many more have two, three and four floors. During the winter the Atlantic wind is extremely strong and the *Rétais* (inhabitants of Ré) have found the safest and best are buildings at ground level. However as the town dwellers became richer on the shipping trade, they demanded taller buildings. But for all their new found ostentation they kept their chimneys small: better safe than buried under one in a gale.

The market hall is in the heart of the town and open every morning. Past the market and up the narrow shopping street of Rue St Mellion you will find the mineral shop at the top selling pretty geological specimens. A little further on and you come to a 350-year old timber frame building, a wine-grower's house. There are some attractive vine decorations carved into the wood, and in keeping, a vine grows up the building, pointing to a weather vane using Halley's Comet as the indicator.

On the way to the church along Place Anatole France are more timber-framed buildings that run into

the Rue du Palais kept shady with old robinia trees. The English destroyed the church and when the Rétais came to rebuild it they were unable to raise enough money to restore it to its original size. Inside look out for the paving stone carved with THOIRAS, and you can go up the tower for a view over the tiles of the town and extensive views of the island.

All through St-Martin, and indeed all over the island in the summer hollyhocks grow wild between the roads and the houses. There are pinks, reds, carmines, whites and almost every variation between. Wander round the narrow streets ensuring you visit the wine merchant in Rue de Sully, who stocks the wines of the Ile de Ré and the local aniseed tasting *Liqueur de Fenouil*.

Leave the town in the direction of La Couade, but carry on past it to the first road signed to Loix. About 765yd (700m) along the little road winding through the salt pans, you come to an unprepossessing building on the left the **Maison du Marais Salant** (Salt Marsh Museum) and for more information see the section Pôles-Nature.

Go on towards **Loix** and at Loix Port the recently restored small tidal mill sits over a small stream; it was originally powered by the ebbing and flowing tides. At the village beware if you decide to drive and not to walk. Many of the roads are so narrow there is only room for one car, and sometimes so narrow you may have to reverse out, unable to drive on.

Steel yourself for these perils. The charm of the whitewashed houses and garden walls, the green shutters and the ever present hollyhocks and wisterias seduce you into mak-

Donkey trousers

In the Maison du Marais Salant, tucked away in a small box on the counter, are some delightful reprints of old postcards of the island showing many features of everyday life. Look for the donkeys in trousers and hats – *Anes en coulottes et chapeaux de jardinier*. The flies and mosquitoes of the salt marshes so annoyed the donkeys that they were wont to run off to escape their tormentors. Unfortunately for their owners, they ran through the vines causing much damage. There was only one solution: hats and trousers!

ing yet more wrong turns until you find yourself utterly and happily lost at the end of a cul-de-sac.

On the way to **Phare des Baleines**, there are often many cyclists. At the *Phare,* the lighthouse, you can go up the 180ft (55m) and 250 steps to the top for extensive views over the island, the Vendée, and the Ile d'Oléron. In 1854 this lighthouse replaced a lantern tower of the seventeenth century that you can still find beyond the present one, and yet beyond that on the rock flats below you, are the old fish traps exposed at low tide.

The Market at Ile de Ré

Tourist Train , Ile de Ré

Round to the right, east, is the **Conche des Baleines**, the 1¹/₂ mile (2.5km) long sandy beach, best approached from one of the three car parks in the forest beside the road from Loix. Here too, on this remote end of the island are clumps of ferns, the source word for the name of the island.

A short way inland from the light-house is the **Arche de Noë** , Noah's Ark, a park of attractions. Divided between indoor and outdoor exhibits you can see the Centre for Breeding Exotic Animals, a butterfly and insect museum, a wax museum of the Ile de Ré Penal Colony, dioramas of naval battles and at the end

Wine tasting

If you like to taste the local wine, the wine growers co-operative is situated at **Le Bois-Plage**, a village with a superb beach at the eastern end of the Anse du Martray. The co-operative's large white buildings are easy to find and they offer a wide range of wines from *vins de table* to sparking wines at warehouse prices. There are *pineaux*, cognacs and the local *Liqueur au Fenouil*.

of the visit concerts given on organs and synthesizers.

The only way from here is back along the spine of the island towards the mainland bridge. On the way stop in **Ars-en-Ré**, classed as 'one of the most beautiful villages in France', with its black and white spired church, used as a beacon for fishermen, and little streets as attractive as those at Loix. At **la Couarde-sur-Mer** is an indoor market in the pedestrianised area of the town.

Two more villages, with narrow lanes between the whitewashed houses are **La-Noue** and **Ste-Marie-de-Ré**. Here the beaches are flat rock with plenty of pools and in a day's exploring you'll find many disused fish traps. Both villages are holiday resorts with hotels, *gîtes* and caravan sites.

To leave the island, follow the signs to the *Viaduc* and then as you reach the mainland, almost immediately pick up the signs for La Rochelle via **La Pallice**, going past the large modern warehouses carrying this name, and on into the dock area. The main imports of La Rochelle are oil and hardwoods, and the main export is grain, witness the large silos.

Follow the road towards the dock, not the *Centre Ville*, and you will go past the old German U-Boat pens with their 23ft (7m) thick roofs, and their 6ft (2m) thick walls. The French have decided that all that concrete is too expensive to destroy, so turning a problem to profit, they let them out to film companies as back-drops. Such films as *The Boat*, a story of a U-Boat widely shown on TV and one of the Indiana Jones adventures are amongst the better known.

TOUR DE LA CHAÎNE, TOUR DE LA LANTERNE, TOUR ST. NICHOLAS

La Rochelle

☎ 05 46 41 74 13.
Open: daily. April to September 10am-7pm, rest of year 10am-12.30pm, 2pm-5.30pm.

MUSÉE GRÉVIN

La Rochelle

Vieux Port towards the Grosse Horlorge.
☎ 05 46 41 08 71.
Open: daily 9am-7pm, June to September till 11pm.

MUSÉE DU FLACON À PARFUM

33 Rue du Temple, La Rochelle
There is no guide, Jean is busy enough in his shop on the ground floor, but each case has a description in English (and 9 more languages too).
☎ 05 46 41 32 40.
Open: Monday 3pm-7pm, Tuesday to Saturday, 10.30am-7pm, July, August, Sundays 3pm-6pm.

MUSÉE DU NOUVEAU MONDE

La Rochelle

☎ 05 46 41 46 50.
Open: Monday to Saturday, closed Tuesday, 10.30am-12.30pm, 1.30pm-6pm, Sundays 3pm-6pm.

Places to Visit

La Rochelle and around

HÔTEL DE VILLE

La Rochelle

The accompanied tour of the interior takes about three-quarters of an hour. Look out for Jean Guiton's Cordovan armchair, the table with his dagger mark and pictures of the siege of 1628.

Open: daily in July to September, weekends from September to June. Reservations via Tourist Office.

THE AQUARIUM

Les Minimes

☎ 05 46 34 00 00.
Open: daily October to March 10am-noon, 2pm-7pm, April to September, 9am-7pm, July and August, 9am-11pm.

MUSÉE DES MODÈLES RÉDUITS

A museum of models of buildings, vehicles and so on...

MUSÉE DES AUTOMATS

Animated models of people and animals.
Both in Rue la Désirée, La Rochelle
☎ 05 46 41 68 08.
Open: June, July, August, 9.30pm-7.30pm, rest of year 10am-noon, 2pm-6pm.

MUSÉE MARITIME

La Rochelle

At the old Fish Market in the Bassin à Flot behind the Quartier Gabut. Outside is the *France I*, an ex-meteorological frigate, Cousteau's famous ship *Calypso*, a fishing trawler and a tug to visit, as well as a number of other smaller vessels. Inside models sailing in an artificial wind, hands-on exhibits, a wind tunnel to walk down – if you can! a submarine adventure, and much, much more plus shops to buy souvenirs.

☎ 05 46 28 03 00.
Open: daily, October to March 2pm-6.30pm, April to September 10am-8pm.

CHURCH, FEUDAL CASTLE AND MAIRIE AT SURGÈRES

Visit via Tourist Office.
☎ 05 46 07 20 02
Open: Tuesday to Saturday 10am-6pm, May to October; rest of year, Tuesday to Thursday, 10am-5pm.

Corderie Royale, Rochefort

ROCHEFORT

This town was built in the seventeenth century when the European maritime nations, particularly Britain and Holland, were starting to expand by carving empires for themselves. France felt she was lagging behind, and Louis XIV worried by the strong British fleet, wanted to establish a secure naval base on the Atlantic coast. He gave his chief minister Jean-Baptiste Colbert, the task and the town of **Rochefort** was established some 9 miles (15km) upstream on the tidal section of the Charente in 1666. Ironically the land was owned by a Protestant aristocrat, and Catholic Louis had to pay an excessive 50,000 crowns both to buy the land and to assuage the aristocrat's conscience!

There was a small village here and the church dating from the 1100's is still in use today. You will find the Tourist Office by the free parking at Cours Roy Bry and the old church at the opposite side.

The Charente at low tide is unnavigable to any ship, and the entrance to the mouth of the river is protected by the islands of Oléron, Aix and Ré, each with a fort to give protection. Other forts were added in the course of time, such as those at Lupin, Boyard, Ile Madame and Saumonards ensuring the British could not attack France's chief naval dockyard.

The land to the south was extremely well wooded and since to build a ship required some 4,000 oaks, it was an added advantage. Upstream at **Ruelle-sur-Touvre**, the Royal Foundry had been established and guns and other iron and bronze parts were brought down by water.

The town was laid out with 14 streets running east-west and 9 streets north-south and giving 61 blocks. Two were not built on, becoming the Place de Colbert and the square in front of the Dockyard, Place de la Gallisonnière. Colbert had decreed that no building should block the end of any road, so that the air was clean and healthy for all. With considerable foresight for 300 years later, each road was to be of 'sufficient width that a carriage could be stopped at either side, and there still be room for two to pass'.

By the end of the following century rich people wanted to make

The building of Rochefort

Twenty thousand workmen both skilled and unskilled, were brought in to build the dockyard. Each artisan was allocated a piece of land measuring 21 x 98ft (6.5 x 30m) where they were to build a house of stone two floors high. The intersections of the streets had better houses of three floors and the elegant iron balconies seen at many first floor windows today are the work of the original dockyard craftsmen.

Rochefort their home, and build town houses there. However the rules that Colbert had laid down 100 years before appeared to preclude any alterations. In the end this was overcome by buying up two or three

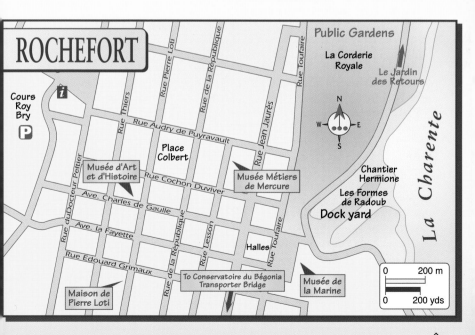

ROCHEFORT

Public Gardens

La Corderie Royale

Le Jardin des Retours

Cours Roy Bry

Rue Thiers

Rue Pierre Loti

Rue de la République

Rue Toufaire

Rue Audry de Puyravault

Rue Jean Jaurès

Place Colbert

Musée d'Art et d'Histoire

Ave. du Docteur Peltier

Rue Cochon Duviver

Musée Métiers de Mercure

Chantier Hermione

Ave. Charles de Gaulle

Ave. la Fayette

Rue Lesson

Les Formes de Radoub

Dock yard

La Charente

Rue Edouard Grimaux

Rue de la République

Halles

Rue Toufaire

Maison de Pierre Loti

To Conservatoire du Bégonia Transporter Bridge

Musée de la Marine

0   200 m

0   200 yds

workers houses and re-building to the new owner's wishes. Examples are the present *Hôtel de Ville* in Place Colbert once the town house of the Marquis d'Anblimont, and on the corner of Rue Pierre Loti and Avenue General de Gaulle is the **Musée de l'Art et d'Histoire.**

It is worth visiting this museum if only to see the 13ft (4m) diameter panoramic model of the town made by M. Touboulic in 1835. It is so detailed that even the parts of the ships in building are shown. There is also a sea-shell room and a picture gallery.

L'Arsenal (the Dockyard) had two dry docks, a number of building slips, a mast mounting dock and fitting out docks. Only the two dry docks remain. The gate to the dry dock on the right is called a boat gate for obvious reasons, and although of immense archaeological importance, was blown up by the Germans at the end of World War II allowing the Charente to flood in. They have both been cleaned and in the other dock you can visit the building of *l'Hermoine*, a copy of the ship that Marquis de Lafayette used to go to Boston in 1780 to support Washington against the British.

Both the Americans and the French see La Fayette as a symbol of liberty and there are some 42 towns in the USA called after him. The new *l'Hermoine* will be an exact replica of the original ship even to the point of ignoring modern safety requirements. It is taking 10 years to complete the project, finishing in 2005, having then a ship 138ft long x 36ft beam (42 x 11m).

Wandering around the streets of Rochefort has its own charms with its many shops and cafés, Place Colbert being well supplied with

Le Musée de la Marine

The Maritime Museum is located in the Fleet Admiral's house right by the entrance to the dockyard. The Museum displays an exceptional collection of ship models from the seventeenth century to today. In addition there are models of wind powered saw mills, cut away sections of ships and other models, arms, cannon, and scrimshaw.

both. In the Place the large statue on the arch is a symbol of the marriage of the Charente with the Atlantic Ocean, taking place by Ile Madame.

In the Rue de Pierre Loti is his house, now a museum to this eccentric mystic. Although he is not well known to English speakers, the house, **Maison de Pierre Loti**, is worth a visit to see the curious rooms and the strange objects he collected. Piere Loti, (1850-1923) the pseudonym of Louis-Marie-Julien Viaud, was a naval captain, who was posted to Turkey and became enamoured of Middle Eastern life.

An exceptional narrator, he wrote a number of novels that are even today taught in French schools. He inherited his father's house and bought the one next door, making changes that caused a considerable stir to the quiet life of Rochefort. The most notable rooms are the renaissance Banqueting Hall which takes most of the height of the building, and where he held his costume balls; the Mosque decorated in material taken from a mosque he

Rope Manufactory

Corderie Royale was built at the same time as the town in 1666 as the premier rope-making factory of the kingdom. The mud here is 98ft (30m) deep and since the building is nearly 440yd (400m) long and built of Crazannes and St Savinien stone, a 'Dutch raft' of 4,000 oak logs had to be laid. The building has had a varied history. It was the rope factory until the war in 1914, when it became part of the mint. In 1926 it was closed, only to be used again as a warehouse by the Germans from 1940 to 1944. At the end of World War II it burnt down and was left derelict until 1967 when at last it became a classified historical monument. Ten years later restoration began, re-opening as a museum in 1986.

Today the museum is called *le Centre International de la Mer*, International Maritime Centre, showing rope making methods through the ages and the construction of the building, all with notices in English. The second part has changing exhibitions always related to the sea.

On Thursdays in July and August, the Tourist Office runs special visits to three of the above attractions with an English speaking guide: L'Hermoine, La Corderie Royale and the House of Pierre Loti. See them for current details.

A place to visit for an hour or so is **Les Métiers de Mercure,** Mercury's Craftsmen – Mercury was the god of shopkeepers. Take a trip back in time and discover Rochefort as it was at the beginning of the century in a collection of seventeen shops and memorabilia set out as a delightful museum.

Transporter bridge

It was never possible to bridge the river because of the height of ship's masts. Only after the decline of Rochefort as a naval base, and the common use of steel in building could the first bridge since Roman times be built. The **Le Pont Transbordeur** was designed and built in 1900 by Ferdinand Arnodin a student of Eiffel. Its use was discontinued in 1966, and it is the last of its type in France, now classified as an historical monument. It has been restored and operates for foot and bicycle passengers but the timetable is complicated so check with the Tourist Office. In its turn it was replaced by a road bridge just down stream (now destroyed) and as traffic further increased the present toll road bridge was built.

found being demolished; a Turkish salon; an Arab bedroom and a Medieval room. Loti is somewhat of a French national figure and the guides, feeling visitors should have full value for their money, spend a long time in each room.

Near the Transporter Bridge in the Rue Charles Plumier is the **Conservatoire du Bégonia,** where some 850 species of begonia are kept and propagated. The begonia was discovered in the West Indies in 1689 by Charles Plumier, a botanist. He named the plant after the then mayor of Rochefort, Michel Begon, though the plant was not introduced into Europe until the end of the next century. The accompanied visit is about an hour and can be arranged for you by the Tourist Office. It is in French, and discusses a large number of varieties in some detail. Questions about the care and propagation of the plant are welcomed, and you can buy specimens while you are there.

Places to Visit

Rochefort

MUSÉE DE L'ART ET D'HISTOIRE

NB Having visited one museum in Rochefort, your ticket entitles you to a reduction at the others.
☎ 05 46 99 83 99
Open: daily, summer 1.30pm-7pm, winter till 5.30pm; closed in winter, Sundays, Mondays and bank holidays.

LE CHANTIER DE L'HERMOINE

Dockyard, Rochefort

☎ 05 46 87 01 90.
Open: July & August 10am-7pm, rest of year 10am-1pm, 2pm-6pm.

LE MUSÉE DE LA MARINE

A ship lover will want to spend at least half a day here; others an hour.
☎ 05 46 99 86 57.
Open: April to September daily 10am-6pm, rest of year 10am-noon, 2pm-5pm; closed 15 November to 15 December.

CORDERIE ROYALE

A tour can be made with an English-speaking guide and there is a large bookshop and a café outside. Allow an hour and a half here.
☎ 05 46 87 01 90.
Open: daily, summer 9am-7pm, winter closes at 6pm. Guided visits available.

MAISON DE PIERRE LOTI

You can follow the fifty-minute visit with a booklet in English.
☎ 05 46 99 16 88.
Open: daily, summer open 10am, guided visits every 30 minutes.

MUSÉE DES MÉTIERS DE MERCURE

☎ 05 46 83 91 50.
Open: summer 10am-8pm, winter 10am-noon, 2pm-6pm; closed Tuesday and Sunday morning.

CONSERVATOIRE DU BÉGONIA

☎ 05 46 99 08 26.
Guided visits only, Tuesday to Saturday 2pm, 3pm, 4pm, 5pm.

The Market at Rochefort

AROUND ROCHEFORT

Tonnay-Charente is most notable for its suspension bridge built in 1842, and the long viaduct leading to it from the south. It is open today only to pedestrians and two-wheeled traffic. The walk across, 223yd (204m) is worthwhile for the view over the tiles of Tonnay, the old docks, towards Rochefort with the new toll bridge and the old transporter bridge. Up stream are views of the Charente and the flood plain carpeted in meadows.

Ile Madame lies beyond Port-des-Barques, a small fishing village. Park by the little Tourist Office with its large sign *'Syndicate d'Initiative'* at the end of the land. You can cross the causeway called the Passe aux Boeufs at falling or low tide. There is a memorial here to the 250 priests

deported to the Ile in 1794. Every August a pilgrimage in their memory crosses to the island.

The crossing will take about 20 minutes, and you will see professional as well as the local oyster and mussel gatherers who are allowed to collect up to 11lb (5kg) per person per day! You can walk round the island taking the road to the right up to the old fort, then follow on to the north-west coast turning back to the south and eventually round to the causeway. From the fort to the north shore you can see Fouras, the Ile d'Aix in the distance to the north-west, the tiny Fort Boyard and the Ile d'Oleron.

Fouras is proud of its situation on its peninsular enabling it to have both a north and a south beach. In the middle of the town is an attractive pedestrianised shopping street, Rue des Halles, with the fish market and the indoor market open every morning. Here you can buy one of the local cheeses, *la Jonchée*.

Special cheese

For over three centuries, since 1683, this delicate cheese has been made in the Rochefort Region from cow's milk following a traditional method. It is prepared in baskets made of rushes gathered from the Rochefort marshes, and kept in fresh water. Only at the time of sale is it removed when almond essence is added. Add sugar to taste before serving. The specialist in Fouras market hall is Bernard Demery. His wife also runs a stall in Rochefort Market Hall and you can buy *la Jonchée* and other local cheeses from her.

At the sea end of this street is Fort Vauban Esplanade where further markets are held on Tuesdays and Fridays from June to September.

Fort Vauban, now missing part of its walls and its barracks, nevertheless presents an imposing site. The Tourist Office is here with a museum on the first floor showing collections of mariners' life and of local history. The crypt is sometimes open where the twelfth-century wells can be seen. From the top, 131ft (40m) above the sea are two viewing tables showing all the major points in view from the mouth of the Charente to the south, past the islands to La Rochelle in the north.

On the road to **Pointe de la Fumée** you pass the Casino and from the Pointe you can take the frequent 20-minute ferry service to the Ile d'Aix. The beach here is distinctly rocky and not suitable for bathing,

although you can walk at low tide to Fort d'Enet about three-quarters of a mile (1.25km) away. Check at the Tourist Office for each day's opening hours, which are dependent on the tides.

Ile d'Aix, the smallest island on the Atlantic Coast, was Napoleon's last home in Europe before being shipped off by the victorious Allies to St Helena in 1815. The ferry service to the island leaves the Pointe de la Fumée at Fouras all year and is seasonal from La Rochelle and Boyardville on the Ile d'Oléron. The town nestles under the walls of the old fortress, with hardly a car to mar the tranquillity, and the small whitewashed houses are dappled with a palette of shades from the hollyhock flowers.

The **Musée Napoléonien** is in the impressive building with its Imperial Eagle and classic columns, built on the orders of Napoleon in 1808. It was here that he stayed during his imprisonment seven years later when he grafted an ash tree onto the elm that can still be seen in the garden. The museum was established in 1925 and contains a record of his life. The **Musée Africaine** is in former barracks and shows ethnic and animal life, using many dioramas.

On your way to Brouage from Rochefort across the former salt marshes there are many birds to be seen both in the air and on the ground. On the way is the **Moëze National Nature Reserve** (see the section Pôles-Nature for details). On the marshes and in the nature reserve you can spot birds of prey that include buzzards, black kite, marsh harriers and kestrel, as well as heron, egret and many varieties of duck. From the Tourist Office in

Island walk

I nstead of visiting a museum on a hot day, take the walk round the island, going beside the beaches, through the woods and past the old fortifications. Give it two or three hours, then before you return to the mainland, you can dine at leisure in one of the restaurants in the town.

Brouage you can buy an illustrated book *Oléron, l'Ile les Chardonnerets* giving details of all the birds to be seen on the island and in the marshes.

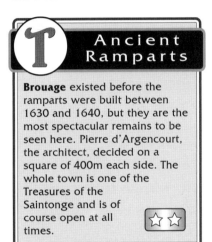

Ancient Ramparts

Brouage existed before the ramparts were built between 1630 and 1640, but they are the most spectacular remains to be seen here. Pierre d'Argencourt, the architect, decided on a square of 400m each side. The whole town is one of the Treasures of the Saintonge and is of course open at all times.

Come to the town from the north and enter by the Porte Royale by the Tourist Office, in the old forge with its huge chimney, in Rue Québec. Start here for a complete circuit going anti-clockwise. Go up the Mancini stairway, so named for Marie Mancini the beloved mistress of Louis XIV. Her father had imprisoned her here in an attempt to keep her from the 'lascivious' clutches of the king!

At the first corner is the **Bastion de la Mer**, an arm of the sea used to reach right to the town from where salt in large quantities was exported. Under the next stairway are the latrines, and the next bastion is St Luc. The southern exit to the town is through the less imposing Porte de Marennes, with the former barracks just inside. The third bastion is named after Cardinal Richelieu, then half way along the eastern wall is the powder store, with the Bastion de la Rivière at the fourth corner. The Halles aux Vivres, food stores, have been restored and are used for exhibitions and as a museum.

In Rue Champlain is a memorial and the family home of Samuel de Champlain, who was born here in 1567 and died in Quebec, the city he founded, in 1635. The church keeps many connections with Canada, always with an exhibition on show, and do not miss the beautiful modern stained glass window.

The Porte Souterraine was the dock where the town could be supplied from the sea under the protection of the town guns. The descriptive placards are also in English.

Continued on page 111...

This 'Focus on Nature' covers 10 Nature Reserves in the department. They have each been given a Quality Charter to ensure their protection, and there are qualified guides on hand during their fixed opening hours. The department is well known for its beaches and coastline, but it has been long concerned about protecting its other riches. With interest increasing in the natural environment these are the first results of its action plan.

1 Ile de Ré: Lilleau des Niges.

Found right at the north of the islands in the *marais salants*, salt marshes, it is a migratory crossroads managed by the LPO (French Bird Protection League), and over 300 species breed and winter here. During the spring and autumn migrations tens of thousands of birds come to the reserve. You can see dunlins, redshanks, and grey plovers mixing with noisy bands of greylag in the old salt-pans. A cycle path runs alongside giving you the chance to approach silently.The Nature Centre is at Les Portes-en-Ré and is open in the summer with exhibitions.

☎: 05 46 29 50 74.

Opening hours: mid-June to mid-September, 10am-12.20pm, 3pm - 7pm. Special visits by appointment.

2 Brouage: Moëze National Nature Reserve.

Situated in the western part of the Brouage Marshes, this is one of the most important sites for migratory and wintering water birds. It is made up of extensive mudflats, that at low tide become the feeding sites for waders and duck. The reserve extends right across to the Ile d'Oléron. Avocets and spoonbills sift the water and the mud for food, wigeon graze the marshes and golden plovers look for worms in the grasslands. At different times of the year you will see greylag geese, teal, pintail, shelduck, black-winged stilt, and bluethroat amongst many more. The Visitor Centre is signposted from Moëze or you can cycle from Brouage.

☎: Espace-Nature 05 46 99 04 36.

Opening hours: mid-June to beginning September on Mondays and Thursdays, 9am - noon, 2pm - 5.30pm. Other times by appointment.

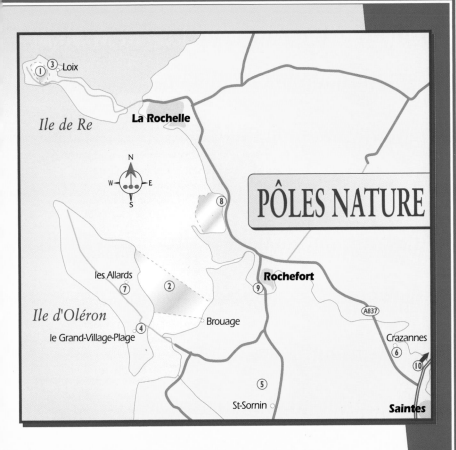

Loix-en-Ré: the Salt Marsh Museum.

Here is the chance to discover the tradition of salt production. In fact if you take a guided visit, you will see the profession of the *saunier*, salt merchant, and after a short initiation, you will be able to extract salt yourself. Salt production on the island dates from the twelfth century, when the monks from the abbey at St-Michel-en-l'Herm, began by building dykes many miles long to defend the salt pans from sea flooding. Salt production lasted until the end of the nineteenth century, when more modern methods took over. The salt here is prized for its trace elements obtained from the clay soil, and the tastier it is the more gourmets appreciate it. More information on this museum is given in the main text. The museum is on the minor road between la Couarde and Loix.

☎: 05 46 29 06 77.

Opening hours: beginning June to end September 10.30am - 12.30pm, 2pm - 7pm.

↑4 Ile d'Oléron: Port-des-Salines at Grand-Village.

The Port-des-Salines is a reconstruction of a traditional village on the Ile d'Oléron. You can see cabins in traditional colours, the old oyster boats tied up and a small port where you can take boat trips. Here too is a salt pan and an old salt warehouse. There is a guided trail to better understand the working of the salt pan and its water system and you are introduced to the local plant life and oyster farming. Port-des-Salines is along the minor road from le Petit-Village.

☎: 05 46 75 82 28.

Opening hours: June to September daily 10.30am - 12.30pm, 3pm - 8pm.

↑5 Saint-Sornin: Maison de Broue.

The Tour de Broue is the *donjon* and all that remains of the feudal castle here. It was built on an 80ft (25m) high promontory over the then Bay of Saintonge, to be a navigation aid and to give protection to the salt pans below. The working of the salt pans, however accelerated the silting up of the Bay. When the shoreline retreated further a new fort had to built at Brouage. The Brouage Marshes are abundant in wildlife, and include such rare creatures as the European pond tortoise, otter, the white egret and the cattle egret. Visits to the marsh are organised, and the development of the Bay is explained though models in the Visitor Centre. Saint-Sornin is off the D728 Marennes-Saintes road. Leave Saint-Sornin for Saint-Symphorien and take the first left at the top of the rise.

☎: 05 46 41 39 04.

Opening hours: daily beginning June to mid-September 3pm - 8pm.

↑6 Crazannes: the Quarry.

The quarry dates from Roman times, the stone being used to build the Arc de Germanicus at Saintes, and quarrying continued until the end of the World War II with the blocks shipped from Port d'Envaux, nearly 2 miles (3km) away. The beautiful cream stone was used in many of the local châteaux as well as Cologne Cathedral, Hôtel des Eleveurs in Brussels, Fort Boyard, and it is said to form the base of the Statue of Liberty. Nature is slowly taking over the quarry with luxuriant vegetation, giving it the sombre air of a half-lit jungle. In the middle of the quarries are some rare species of broom, the spectacular fern, *scolopendra*, and the nightjar is often to be seen. Approach from the Aire de la Pierre de Crazannes on the A 837 motorway, or signposted from the D119 Saint-Savinien to Plassay road.

☎:05 46 91 83 66

Opening hours: daily October to May 10am - noon, 2pm - 5pm, June to September 9am - 7pm.

↑7 Ile d'Oleron: Marais aux Oiseaux et Parc Animalier.

In this discovery park you will find both wild and domestic animals and birds. There are over 60 species and 500 animals, some endangered and mostly those of the fenlands and including coypu and deer. The arrangements allow you to get to know animals and birds that are normally difficult to see and identify in the wild. The visit starts with a mini-farm, donkeys, goats, rabbits, and goes onto spoonbills little egrets and even owls. There are information panels at each hide in this educative visit. The centre also tends to animals and birds wounded in accidents with cars or electric lines, or after being oiled, starved and hunted. Signposted from the main island road just over a mile (2km) north-west of Dolus d'Oléron.

☎: 05 46 75 37 54.

Opening hours: open all year round, in July and August daily 10am - 8pm.

↑8 Chatelaillon-Plage: Marais d'Yves National Nature Reserve.

This important nature reserve of nearly 500 acres (194 hectares) along one of the principal migration routes of Europe, covers dunes, marshes and a huge lagoon used as a resting site for dozens of species of bird. The marsh was gradually formed as successive banks of sand blocked the outflow of the little stream, the Gères, and now the latest line of dunes encloses the brackish water of a large lagoon. Greylag, ducks and heron species, white storks and a variety of waders can be seen though the seasons. Management of the site is necessary, the biodiversity is one of the highest in France, and while Highland cattle and horses maintain the grasslands, water levels are controlled by solar-powered pumps. The Visitor Centre at Marouillet has exhibitions and a large bay window giving a fine view across the lagoon. The LPO organises regular guided visits to the reserve's hides. Best approached from the Aire de Marouillet off the southbound carriageway of the N137 la Rochelle to Rochefort road.

☎: Espace-Nature 05 46 99 04 36.

Opening hours: open all year. July to mid-September 10am - noon, 3pm - 7pm. Short visits at 10am, 11am, 3pm, 4pm, 5pm, 6pm. Longer visits by appointment.

↑9 Rochefort: Station de Lagunage.

The waste water of the town is treated with the help of nature to produce water of a quality good enough for bathing, for the production of oysters and to make a home to thousands of birds in these lagoons. In 1987 the town decided to take an ecological approach to the treatment of its waste water and built the site covering 90 acres (35 hectares). The water is circulated through several lagoons where it is re-oxygenated by wind and sun. The residual sediments are used as fertilisers for the town's parks, and the methane produced by fermentation generates electricity for the pumps on the site. Birds to be seen include the pygmy cormorant, black tern and the shoveller duck. Situated and signposted on the town side of the toll bridge over the Charente.

☎: Espace-Nature 05 46 99 04 36.

Opening hours: mid-July to beginning September Monday to Friday 2pm - 6pm. Other times guided visits by appointment.

↑10 Dampierre-sur-Boutonne: Maison de l'Ane du Poitou (the National Donkey Stud).

The stud was created in 1980 to prevent the extinction of the oldest donkey breed in the world. A new breeding herd was founded by out-breeding with the closely related Portuguese ass, and an inventory was made of pure bred individuals. This has born fruit since there are now 260 *baudets*, from a total in 1980 of only 60. The *Baudet du Poitou*, is a large and almost teddy-bear-looking donkey. The visit comprises a small but thorough exhibition, a short film, then a visit into the fields amongst all the donkeys and horses, with no-one rushing you to leave. The *baudet* is the most friendly of all donkeys and you should not miss the opportunity to pat them and talk to them. In the past they carried a reputation for being thoroughly bad tempered but these days with better treatment and an easier life, they respond positively to friendship. Allow up to an hour. From the D950 Melle to St-Jean-d'Angely road, and at la Villedieu take the D115 towards Dampierre-sur-Boutonne. In $2\frac{1}{2}$ miles (4km) follow the sign posts.

☎: 05 46 24 07 72.

Opening hours: open all year, every day from beginning April to end September 10am - noon, 2pm - 7pm, July and August, 10am - 7pm.

Many of the sites are open outside the popular times shown. For details telephone Espace-Nature 05 46 99 04 36.

ILE D'OLERON, THE ISLAND OF LIGHT

Allow a full day for this introductory drive. Justly called the Isle of Light, Oléron has so many of the features that go to make an enjoyable holiday. The beaches are sandy, long, wide and very warm; the towns are small and comfortable, there are forts to see, a forest tramway to travel on, bicycles and horses to ride, boats and surf-boards to sail and almost every manner of sport to take part in.

Drive straight onto the island over the magnificent viaduct, over 2 miles (3km) long and toll free. As you come onto the island turn right for **Chateau-d'Oléron** and you will be immediately impressed with the citadel built by Vauban to guard the mouth of the Charente, in 1666. Drive round and park near the Citadel.

La Cotinière, Ile d'Oleron

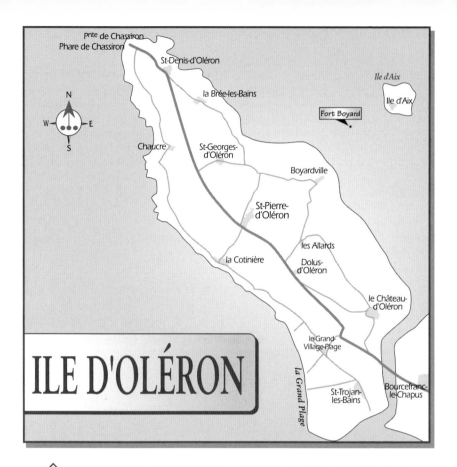

ILE D'OLÉRON

Map labels:
pnte de Chassiron
Phare de Chassiron
St-Dènis-d'Oléron
la Brée-les-Bains
Ile d'Aix
Ile d'Aix
Fort Boyard
Chaucre
St-Georges-d'Oléron
Boyardville
St-Pierre-d'Oléron
les Allards
la Cotinière
Dolus-d'Oléron
le Château-d'Oléron
le Grand-Village-Plage
la Grand Plage
St-Trojan-les-Bains
Bourcefranc-le-Chapus

The Citadel at Chateau-d'Oléron

It was reinforced at the end of the seventeenth century but was damaged in bombardments during the liberation of the island in April 1945. The Tourist Office in the town will supply you with a plan of the citadel or you can take the 35-minute tourist train ride, with a commentary in French. Even though it is somewhat ruined, there is still plenty to see and do including a museum and temporary exhibitions. You can climb the ramparts, allow the children to play on the wide grassy slopes, explore the caverns in the walls, or just walk round and think about the work that went into its building and manning. There are two viewing tables to help you identify the many parts of the Citadel and from the ramparts are views of the viaduct and the mainland.

The busy thriving town of **Chateau-d'Oléron** lies within the outer fortifications with a pedestrian zone full of small shops and cafés. Near the sea entrance to the port is the **Musée d'Ostréicole** featuring the oyster industry. A popular dish is the *Eclade*, a delicious concoction of mussels cooked on pine needles.

Leave the town by the western exit. Following the signs of the Routes des Huîtres. This will take you north along the coast with views of the oyster beds in the **Réserve Naturelle de Moëze**, see Pôle-Nature section, alternating with tree covered dunes.

In about 3 miles (5km) at the signs to Port-d'Arceau, turn left to Les Allards and pick up the signs to the **Marais aux Oiseaux et Parc Animalier** a short distance away. (For details see Pôles-Nature section.)

Return to Les Allards and on to **Boyardville**, so named after the town built for the workers who themselves built Fort Boyard about 2 miles (3.5km) out in the channel, and although it cannot be visited, most boat trips sail close by. The Fort is used as a TV studio for gameshows, on both UK and European TV.

The commercial dock is in the river cut, and in town the marina is surrounded by a charming square of cafés and shops. Leave the square by the left-hand end of the market and follow the signs to **Les Saumonards** about $1^1/_2$ miles (2km) away. The embarkation point to the Ile d'Aix (see above) is on the way. At the end of the road is a magnificent sandy beach stretching some 3 miles (4.5km) to the west.

Continue the drive by returning the way you came and make for St-Georges. But on leaving Sauzelle turn right for Foulerot and make your way through the holiday towns of **la Brée-les-Bains** and **St-Denis-d'Oléron** to the **Pointe de Chassiron** and the lighthouse at the northern tip of the island.

Phare de Chassiron

The top of the lighthouse is 224 steps and 160ft (50m) above and the panorama reaches round to the Antioche rocks to the north east, the Iles d'Ré and Aix, La Rochelle and back across Ile d'Oléron itself. At low tide on the beach below you can find the remains of the fish traps used by the Oléronais into this century. The low walls allowed the fish to come in at high tide and they were trapped as it fell.

Leaving the lighthouse go to the crossroads and turn right along the west side of the island above the low eroding cliffs to Chaucre and onto the main road to Cheray. Turn right here to the beach at **les Sables-Vignier** where, with a south or east wind, the beach is soft and balmy, while in the west wind the waves crash on the sand.

Back again now to **St-Georges** for the old market hall and its church. Look for the large sundial opposite the Tourist Office and see if you can spot the dog in the carvings to the west door. Leave town for **St-Pierre**, the largest town on the island, where the only reasons for coming are the Tourist Office, the banks in Place Gambetta and the supermarkets on the outskirts.

Drive over the main road towards **La Cotinière**, the main fishing port of the island. Just over half a mile (1km) from St-Pierre is the **Parc d'Oiseaux**, with over 200 varieties of European and worldwide species of birds.

La Cotinière is extremely bright with gaily painted boats in the sheltered fishing port packed with pleasure cruisers and sailing boats. The jetties, the lighthouse and the cafés all add to the pleasant scene. The fish auction, *La Criée*, can be watched at 7am and at 4pm. You will also find an Aquarium and a market, where you can buy good *Pineau des Charentes* at bargain prices.

Pineau des Charentes

The story goes that in the sixteenth century, a wine grower accidentally poured some wine must into a barrel containing a quantity of cognac, then seeing his mistake, and with disgust at the waste of both products pushed the barrel into a corner of his *chais*. Years later, after a bumper harvest, he needed every barrel he could lay his hands on, and he pulled this one out of its corner.

He was on the point of emptying it away when he thought to taste the contents and was pleasantly surprised. Thus was born *Pineau des Charentes*. In fact these days, for a bottle of *Pineau* to have its *appellation* the wine must have a minimum of 10 per cent alcohol, with the added cognac raising it to a minimum of 16.5 per cent.

The French like you to drink it extremely cold – as low as two or three degrees Celsius – if you cannot get it as low as that, drink it at room temperature, since at five to ten degrees you will see little improvement. It comes either white, red or rosé and many believe the rosé to be the best.

It must be said that the one-way system is not a help to getting into the middle of the village, and having got there, you may have difficulty finding parking. But it is attractive and worth the effort.

Leave La Cotinière towards Vert-Bois to the south along the coast road. After $4\frac{1}{2}$ miles (7km) turn right to **Vert-Bois-Plage** through the pine woods to the large parking areas by the beach. You are at the northern end of the $5\frac{1}{2}$ mile (9km) sandy **Grande Plage**, 110yd (100m) wide at high tide and extending to 650yd (600m) and more at low.

Return to the main road and turn right for **Le Grand-Village**. Turning right again into the road to *La Plage* you will find the **Maison Paysanne Oléronaise**, a museum to the peasant life in the last century. The local History Society has built a house, a forge and various other buildings in a genuine reproduction of peasant style including four-poster bed with the occupants sitting up. They always slept this way, since the only people to lay flat were the dead!

It is all set pleasantly within a quarter hectare (an acre) of woodland right in the heart of the village, with a two-roomed museum of traditional Oléron coifs and clothes. The traditional occupation of the island was the production of salt by evaporation. So much was produced this way that there was a thriving market to northern Europe. The trade though, was destroyed in the religious wars of the late 1500s, and the enterprising Oléronais used the salt pans as *claires* to raise oysters.

La Cotinière, Ile d'Oleron

Record of payment

On your travels round the region you will see stones jutting out of the walls of the older houses like the house here. The mason building the house set a stone out every time he was paid so the fewer off-set stones you had in your wall the more your care with money was stated for all time!

Return for **St-Trojan** passing along one side of the St-Trojan Forest with its many miles of walks and cycle paths. The attractive open-planned town boasts some nice beaches sheltered from any westerly winds, and every March the Festival of Mimosa is held. Close to the middle is the *Petit Train Touristique* that runs twelve times a day each way in the summer to the southern end of the Grande Plage.

Just by the main road is the little port, situated about $1^{1}/_{2}$ miles (2km) up a winding channel from the sea. Nearby are signs to the Port des Salines, a reconstruction of a traditional village, (see the section Pôles Nature for details). If you haven't been thoroughly bewitched into staying on this, the largest of the French Atlantic islands, return to La Grand-Village-Plage and follow the signs marked *Le Viaduc*.

ESTUARY OF THE SEUDRE, OYSTER COUNTRY AND SAND DUNES

Allow most of a day for this drive, all day if you decide to spend time on Ronce-les-Bains beaches. You will be visiting the Forêt de la Coubre and the Côte Sauvage, the oyster capital of the Atlantic Coast and a beautiful small château.

Start at **Saujon**, a small and pretty town about 6 miles (9.6km) inland from Royan. It is thriving, with a well-shopped main street, and is home to a preserved tourist railway running on steam and diesel from Saujon to La Tremblade 15 miles (24km) away. The Tourist Office in the shady main square has the current year's timetable.

Take the D14 towards La Tremblade. At the roundabout is the Co-operative de la Seudre selling all local brandies, *Pineaux* and wines, and well worth the visit. Take the first exit here and in three-quarters of a mile (1km) turn left along the minor road signed to **Mornac-sur-Seudre**. Mornac itself is a pretty tangle of tiny streets containing oyster fishermen's houses, craft shops of potters and a silk weaver, and an attractive stone-built *Halle*, market hall.

The D14 takes you to **La Tremblade**. In the Tourist Office you can see a half-hour video presentation with English handout on the culture and harvesting of oysters. Here too, is a Maritime Museum, along the Rue de la Gare, and the other end of the tourist railway. You can follow this road signed *Ostréiculture* taking you almost into the middle of the estuary to see the oyster fishermen and their cabins.

Leave La Tremblade for **Ronce-les-Bains**, an attractive seaside village with sandy beaches. There are views from here to the Pointe de Chapus, and over the Pertuis de Maumusson to Ile d'Oléron. You can spend time on the sandy beaches then follow the main road signed to Royan via the Forest.

Forêt de la Coubre

After 4 miles (6km) of driving through the **Forêt de la Coubre**, you come to the **Tour du Gardout** on the left, with panoramic views over the forest. The forest has fixed the dunes of the **Côte d'Avert** more usually called the **Côte Sauvage**. Although there are many car parks along the road with paths leading to the beaches **be warned bathing is forbidden in the cold and dangerous water.** The fortifications you see from time to time were put up by the Germans in World War II.

Five miles further on you will come to the signposts for the **Phare de la Coubre** and you can park adjacent to it. There are in fact two lighthouses here, only the nearest to the sea open to visitors. It has been rebuilt many times because of the movement of the sands, and is one of the most powerful lights in France, with a range of 30 miles (45km). The 300 steps up the metal stairs lead you to an amazing panoramic view reaching from the south west, the Phare de Corduan in the sea, the Pointe de Grave on the far side of the Gironde Estuary, to

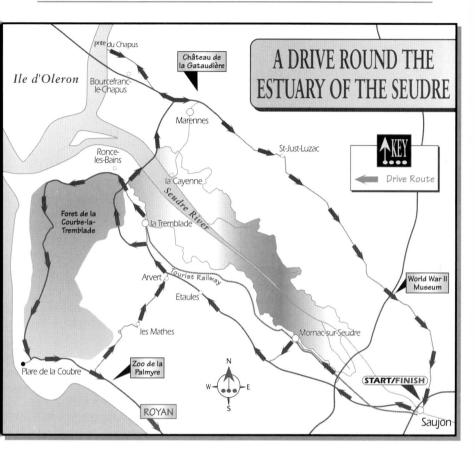

A DRIVE ROUND THE ESTUARY OF THE SEUDRE

Map labels: pnte du Chapus · Ile d'Oleron · Bourcefranc-le-Chapus · Château de la Gataudière · Marennes · St-Just-Luzac · Ronce-les-Bains · la Cayenne · Seudre River · KEY · Drive Route · Foret de la Courbe-la-Tremblade · la Tremblade · Arvert · Tourist Railway · Etaules · World War II Museum · les Mathes · Mornac-sur-Seudre · Plare de la Coubre · Zoo de la Palmyre · N W E S · START/FINISH · ROYAN · Saujon

Royan and the long spit of sand close at hand. Continue your drive towards Royan.

At La Palmyre on the way to St-Palais-sur-Mer is the the Palmyre Zoo, over 30 acres (12 hectares) in extent, and managing to pack in over 1,000 animals of many species. There is a gentle routeing system that ensures you see every animal, bird and reptile. Seals perform twice a day in a large blue and white tiled pool. Parrots are put through their paces by their keepers in a second 'theatre'. Zoos can be contentious these days, and if a criterion of the well being of the animals is their willingness to breed in captivity, then they are well cared for. It is the big cats who are least happy with their lot, finding the spaces allowed them rather small.

Take the D141 to Arvert where turn to bypass La Tremblade for the road to Marennes over the bridge. On the right you have a panoramic view of the whole 10 miles (16km) of the estuary of the River Seudre, with the boats plying back and forth. You will need to drive slowly to appreciate it all – even if this means annoying impatient French drivers!

Marennes is the most famous region in France for oysters, the specialty being the much sought after Green Oyster. The town church is

war, when it took eighteen months to complete. The sitting room has stone walls carved with emblems showing the sciences, the arts and the seasons. The bronze chandelier in this room weighs 660lb (300kg) and was the only item of furniture not taken away and walled up when the Germans invaded in 1940. Outside, the west front is the most decorated and should be seen in late afternoon light to best appreciate its beauty.

Interestingly, the roof has both tiles and slates, and unlike many châteaux in France, there is no lake in the grounds. During the winter the land becomes waterlogged, and in order to have a view of water François Freneau cleared all the trees to the west for a view of both the sea and Ile d'Oleron. Today the trees have re-grown.

Back at the main road take the D728 towards Saintes. Turn off to St-Just-Luzac for the model Railway Museum just behind the church. It has over 2,500 locomotives with rolling stock and other pieces, both French and foreign, some dating back to 1875. Continue with the D728 and in 3 miles (5km) fork right to Le Gua. After a visit to the Musée de la Poche de Royan, World War II Museum go through Le Gua and back to Saujon.

Of considerable military interest, the museum shows shows the final winkling out of the Germans from the Royan Pocket right at the end of World War II in April 1945 (see below). It has authentic German and American vehicles, small arms and heavy guns, uniforms dressed onto models along 394ft (120m) of diorama and a very wide variety of ammunition and equipment. Panels of original photographs showing the district from the air, the action and the resulting destruction of the Royan area are on display.

Some British visitors wonder why there are no British soldiers and equipment shown. As the owner is keen to point out, British troops were busy defeating the German Armies in the north at this time and only the French and US Forces were involved, though the RAF did carry out a number of raids.

ROYAN

The southernmost of all the superb resorts stretching from St-Brévin-les-Pins on the mouth of the Loire to here at the mouth of the Gironde. Running into each other are the sister resorts of **St-Georges-de-Didonne, Pontaillac** and **St-Palais-sur-Mer**. Royan and St-Georges have big wide sandy beaches locally called *conches*, each $1^1/_2$ miles (2.5km) long, and Pontaillac and St-Palais-sur-Mer have sandy coves. The local Royan sardine that is much appreciated by gastronomes, you will find on sale in the town.

At the end of the World War II the German garrison decided to hold out against the Allied forces, with the result that almost all the buildings were destroyed, and it was not liberated until the final days of the war in April and May 1945.

The beach at **Royan** curves to face south and south west, la Grande Conche, catching the sun almost all day long, and the low tide leaves it over 880yd (800m) wide along much of its length. One Tourist Office is here right by the front and a second is in the Palais des Congrès. There are restaurants, ice cream shops and a French Punch and Judy show at the Royan end, and as the beach stretches towards St Georges it is backed by small hotels and private houses.

In the town of Royan, the main shopping street is the plane tree lined Rue Aristide Briant, with the central market at the top; there are more shops in the Boulevard de la Republique, Rue Gambetta, along the front and in the Port de Plaisance.

Royan Cathedral

The cathedral was a casualty of the war, and has been rebuilt to a modern design in pre-stressed concrete covered in resin to protect it from the weather. The pity is this has not been entirely successful; the steel peeks through in places, and the building leaks in the rain. The stained glass windows are worth seeing, as is the wide vault of the roof supported only by the walls. Despite the errors quickly revealed in the fabric, the architect, Guillaume Gillet was given the accolade of being buried here, and even a Humanist like the author, cannot fail to be moved by this inspiring cathedral.

Each day at 4pm (Mondays 3.30pm) The *Criée*, fish auction, takes place at the port. You can watch the 'shout' from the special public gallery, the negotiation between the wholesale fish merchant and the auctioneer. Watch especially for the sale of the 'noble' fish, those appreciated by gourmets, including turbot, sole, bass, skate, gilthead, devilfish and *côteau*, a Gironde speciality.

You can take boat trips up and down the coast to a variety of places including the Zoo at La Palmyre, the Lighthouse of Cordouan and fishing trips; timetables from the Tourist Offices. A wander round the Port de Plaisance and the shops here, stopping at one of the cafés is pleasantly relaxing.

There are a number of tennis courts throughout the resorts, as well as horse riding in the country and along the beaches. You can walk along the Corniche leaving from the port past the Palais des Congrès and follow the coast along to Pontaillac. There are two sandy *conches* to walk round, Chay and Pigeonnier, before you reach the Conche de Pontaillac about an hour later. Here the bay is larger and at the far end is the Casino. You can continue your walk along the low cliffs and round the *conches* all the way past St-Palais-sur-Mer to the **Phare-de-Terre-Nègre** lighthouse, following the waymarked GR4 long distance footpath. There are sea views, the Corduan Lighthouse on the horizon and the fishermen's huts and square nets, *carrelets*. Return on foot or by bus.

Port de Plaisance, Royan

SAINTES:
THE ROMAN TOWN

In Roman times **Saintes** was called *Mediolanum Santorum* – The Market Town of the Santones people – and from Santones the modern name of both the town and the district of Saintonge comes. Today, when you move away from the hum of modern traffic, you could almost be stepping back to Roman times with the pantiled roofs and narrow lanes.

As the provincial capital of Aquitaine it became one of the major Roman towns, close in importance to Lyons, the capital of all Gaul. It is steeped in Roman history, and can claim to be the town with the best and most important Roman

Arc de Germanicus

The arch was erected at the beginning of the first century AD on the left bank at the entrance to a bridge over the Charente. In 1843 after the demolition of the bridge, Prosper Merimée the author, saved the arch by having it reconstructed in its present position on the right bank. The inscriptions on the upper part dedicate it to the Emperor Tiberius and to Germanicus and Drusus. However the real hero of the piece is one Caius Julius Rufus who actually paid for its original construction, and if you look carefully you can see his dedication.

remains outside Provence and the Rhône Valley.

Now for modern Saintes: the Tourist Office is along the Cours National in the Villa Musso, an attractive town house built at the end of the last century. You will find the biggest shops along the Avenue Gambetta and the Cours National but the real interest lies to the south of this axis. Pont B. Palissy over the River Charente, divides the two streets, and you can park on the east side of the bridge at Place Bassompierre and near the **Arc de Germanicus**.

A short way from the Arc de Germanicus is the **Archaeological Museum** with no entry charge. The Museum is in two parts: in the Bureau d'Acceuil showing the more interesting parts of Roman life, and in the building a few yards away, the old abattoir built of the beautiful local stone, showing the major works recovered in the course of excavations.

Saintes is best appreciated on foot. From the Archaeological Museum cross the Charente by the footbridge, and into the Rue St Pierre opposite, leading to the cathedral. A market is held on most Mondays here.

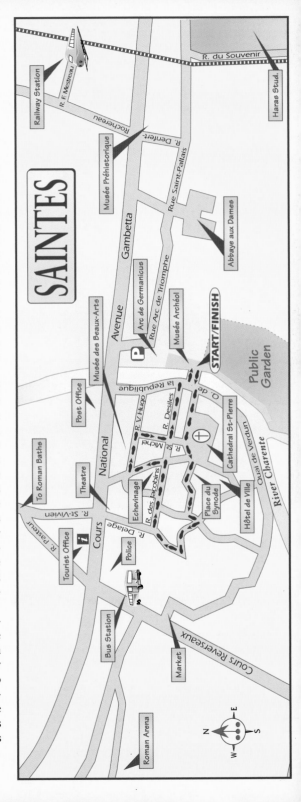

SAINTES

Leave the Place du Synode, opposite, by the further left hand exit to the Square des Nivelles, a pleasant city garden behind the *Hôtel de Ville*. Leave this also by its top left hand corner into Rue Charles Dangibaud and the Ruelle de l'Hospice up the steps to the top with a good view behind you. Drop down the little Rue des Jacobins, to the municipal library where it is worth stepping into the tree ringed courtyard for a moment.

At the end of the street, turn left into the Rue Alsace Lorraine for the **Musée des Beaux Arts** at the Echevinage where there are works by Breugel, Copignet, Schooten and a room of local pottery. A few steps further on go into Rue Victor Hugo, with a splendid townscape behind you of the street and the cathedral.

Not far the other way is the Palais de Justice and opposite is the city theatre. Ahead down the Rue Victor Hugo, on the alignment of the Roman *Decumanus Maximus*, the main east-west street, is the second part of the Musés des Beaux Arts at the Presidial. Turn right along Rue Saint Michel, then left into Rue Désiles to a small section of the Roman third century ramparts. At the end of the street is the Quai de Verdun. Go right, away from the main road bridge, and past the many attractive town houses with their gardens and wrought iron balconies. Return to the footbridge and your car.

The **Roman Baths** and the **Arena** are open all through the day and are within easy walking distance of the Tourist Office. Turn right on leaving the Tourist Office and right again into Rue Pasteur, then on the left is the Rue des Thermes Romains with the remains about 55yd (50m)

further on at the top of the hill. You will find a helpful display board on the site. The most visual remain is that of the *Caldarium*, or hot bath, with its statue at the front, measuring about 30 x 60ft (10 x 20m).

Return the way you have come and cross into the Cours Reverseaux with its daily market. On the other side of the road, by the trees, steps lead down to the Avenue des Arènes, a wide grass-covered way about 275yd (250m) long, between the well kept gardens of the residents whose houses are at the top of the valley sides. Many have been planted and decorated in keeping with the Roman atmosphere.

On the east side of the river and some 220yd (200m) further east from the Arc Germanicus is the **Abbaye Aux Dames**, used today as a concert venue for all types of music. From the time it was founded in 1047, the abbess was chosen only from amongst the most illustrious families of France. She was given the title Madame de Saintes and from her came the name of the Abbey. Architecturally it stands in its own right; culturally it is the heart of Saintes. In July the *Académies Musicales de Saintes*, a major classical music cycle is held, with other local music festivals and exhibitions throughout the year.

A little further on near the junction of the Niort and Cognac roads is the **Haras National**: a part of the National Stud. There are more than 60 horses here including thoroughbred English, Arab, heavy Breton draught horses and the charming donkey, the *Baudet* of Poitou. You will find more details of the Haras National under la Roche-sur-Yon in the Vendée chapter.

Roman Arena at Saintes

A s you round a slight bend the main entrance to the Arena comes dramatically into view. You can perhaps imagine the throngs of people and the cheers of the crowd who had come here for their entertainment.

Go into the Arena itself, used these days for less spectacular diversions and make your way round the left hand side to the top where there are two display boards, with information in English as well as French. The Arena was built between 40 and 50 AD in the reign of Emperor Claudius and its remains are the most impressive of the Roman city. Despite it being used as a stone quarry in the middle ages, it is still one of the best preserved monuments of its type in the whole of France. Once it had a capacity of 20,000, drawing the population from the countryside as well as the town.

The builders had chosen this site to keep the cost down with the western seating using the valley side as support, and those on the east resting on arches. Leave the way you have come, and if you wish you can turn right out of the Avenue des Arènes with the St Eutrope Church towering above you and dedicated to the first bishop of Saintes.

AROUND SAINTES

On the D131 at **la Chapelle-des-Pots** is a museum to pottery, craftsmen pot makers in the village, and a larger factory about one mile out of town to the east. There have been potters here since around 1250 when it became known as La Chapelle des Potiers (Potters' Chapel), then later it took on its present name meaning Pots' Chapel! But here were high quality clays, a forest to supply the fuel, and the River Charente close by to safely ship the goods out.

In the beginning only utilitarian goods were produced but by the Renaissance decorative objects were

All that is left of the feudal castle is the Ogival Room, named from the shape of its arch. You enter it down steps at the front of the château and go down about 20ft (6m). In the buildings forming the right of the courtyard is a good collection of local furniture, implements and artifacts. Eight rooms show life as it was in the 150 years before the World War I.

Park on the outskirts and go into the town along Rue Pascal-Bourcy and towards the Grosse Horloge straddling the street called after it. The clock was put there in 1332 and the bell, called *le Sin*, from the Latin *signum*, a sign, was used initially to sound at the time the town gates were closed and for other important events.

The Market Hall is along Rue Hôtel de Ville to your right. Go under the tower to the Place du Pilori, and the Fontaine du Pilori. The original inscription reads 'In the year 1546 I was built and put in place'. In 1819 the owner of the Château at Brizambourg ($9^1/_2$ miles [16km] to the south-east) gave this well covering to the town, and it was placed over the well normally used only in time of siege.

The main shopping street, Rue Gambetta has a number of half-timbered buildings and at its end turn into Rue de Minage to the **Abbaye Royale**. The Abbey, is now a school, and in the *Court d'Honneur* the *Acceuil*, Reception, is on the left side where you can arrange a tour of the bell towers of the Abbey with their views of the countryside. In the Rue de Verdun the Museum has the Citroën Black and Yellow Cruisers and a Silver Crescent half-track car, that crossed the Sahara in 1921.

Leave St Jean d'Angely south on the N150 and just before you come to the end of the houses take the Taillebourg road,

St-Jean-d'Angely

St-Jean-d'Angely is always signposted St-Jean-d'Y and the name conjures a romantic town, and it has a lot more half timbered houses than most towns in the Saintonge, and a nice shopping area in the midst of both broad and narrow streets. The Tourist Office is in the Rue de la Grosse Horloge and opposite the Fontaine du Pilori.

and follow the signs to the **Château Beaufief** about 2 miles (3km) away.

History of Château Beaufief

In 1768 when the house was built, Auguste Perraudeau bought 1,500 acres (600 hectares) of land stretching from the house to the edge of St-Jean-d'Angely. He and his descendants lived there for the next 226 years, with a small intermission during the French Revolution. There had been a fine stand of oaks outside the main gate, but like many châteaux, this one was taken over in World War II by the Germans who did not treat it kindly, cutting down the oaks for heating. The buildings fell in to alarming disrepair after the war, and since 1977 the restoration has been continuous.

The present owners, M and Mme Bonvalet, acquired the château in the early 1990s. From the 600 hectares 200 years ago, there are only three left to the property today, and behind the château is also the St-Jean-d'Angely exercise field that is permanently open.

Inside the main entrance the attractive curving flight of stairs, with wrought iron banisters dating from the eighteenth century, lead to a double bay on the landing. The black and white tiles are original and the hall was heated in the Roman fashion of hot air under-floor conduits to be seen at the foot of the stairs.

The drawing room on the first floor is parquet in light oak with a pleasing triple string of hardwood round the edges and the shutters, like English ones of the same period, are on the inside. The front window has the magnificent view up the drive, past the lawns and flower beds to the gates, and the rear windows look out over the old trees in the park. This tall cool blue room, has Masonic devices and decorations of agriculture. The mirror, above the fireplace of green Norwegian marble, has been kept to show the two bullet holes made by the occupying Germans.

Outside the pretty little chapel between the house and the old brandy cellars (now used as an exhibition room) has interesting plaster casts on the wall and an altar made of the beautiful white Crazannes stone.

Walk round first to the priest's garden, called so, not because it was the priest's, but because it was all shrubs and needed little tending. Priests being so busy they did not have time to tend their gardens! The walled kitchen garden leads to the old servants quarters, now a pretty rose clad cottage with a 82ft (25m) deep well in front, whose diameter at the top is twice that at the bottom. Behind the château, though no longer belonging to it, is the old *Pigeonnier* now used as a home.

Beyond St Jean on the D950 is the little town of **Aulnay**. The church is near the main road, away from the middle of the town, and close to the Tourist Office. In contrast to most French churches the graveyard here surrounds it and is full of medieval gravestones. The west end and especially the south wall have beautifully carved doorways. Inside is worth a visit (guided tours available) with stained glass windows and carved capitals on the pillars. Look out for the famous elephants with the inscription '*Hi sunte elephantes*', 'Here are elephants'. Across the main road from Aulnay and along the minor roads is **Dampierre-sur-Boutonne** and its renaissance château.

On your way back towards Aulnay and in St-Georges-de-Longuepierre take the signs to the **Angélique Confiserie.** Follow these for about 2 miles (3km) to Petit-Oulme where Jean-Yves and Monique Pluchon grow their own angelica, candy it and sell it. You can see the full process from the angelica growing in the fields, the preservation described by Monique herself, to the results in sticks of candied angelica, cut and sugared, chocolate covered, with almonds and so on. She will of course allow you to buy these delicious products of hers after you have sampled them. Monique will tell you that angelica likes its 'roots deep in the ground and its head high in the sky', and grows about as tall as she herself – 5ft 3in (1.60m).

North-west of Saintes lies the **Château de Panloy.** This small château is a double winged house of two floors dating from the mid-1700s that looks towards the River Charente. The hunting gallery has some tens of deer heads from the forests around Poitiers where the Dukes of Graille had their winter residence, staying at Panloy during the summer. The drawing room is

Château Dampierre-sur-Boutonne

The château was built between 1495 and 1515 on an island surrounded by the tiny Boutonne river, a stream really. It is most interesting for its two galleries and its upper hall where all the owners are listed, from Adalbert at the end of the tenth century to the present day, Jean-Louis Hedelin. The lower gallery ceiling is divided into sixty odd, plain, uncarved sections, but the upper gallery is a veritable alchemist's book of spells. Each panel is carved with arcane devices and while some are pristine others have suffered over time. Should you wish to delve more deeply into their meanings a full description of each is displayed in the ticket office.

Château de la Roche-Caurbon

hung with important and valuable Beauvais tapestries and the dining room, in common with the rest of the house, has original furniture. The huge dovecote has a revolving ladder for ease of reaching the birds, and the stables and laundry are shown in their original form.

A short distance away is another *Trésoir*, the **Château de Crazannes,** built of the local, and very famous, stone. The approach is along a small avenue of lime trees and you can still see the moats, a tower and a drawbridge of the old feudal castle. The ornamented renaissance door leads into the Great Hall decorated in carved wood and with a magnificent fireplace.

The view of the River Charente from the road at **St-Savinien** is quite charming as it curves to the left among the willow trees, and until the eighteenth century the river provided a living for *patageux,* fishers of mussels for pearls. The road runs about three-quarters of a mile (1km) towards Rochefort where it has been set out in a most attractive manner. The medieval part of St-Savinien is the maze of steep narrow lanes leading up to the church on the crown of the hill.

Just to the south-west of here is possibly the most beautiful château in south-western France, **Château de la Roche-Corbon.** Before you reach the house, you can go up into the gatehouse to the little museum of pre-history with a collection of material found by the family, mainly from the grounds. (See box on the History of the Château on page 132).

The tour of the house starts in the hall with its creamy-white curving staircase, tapestries and pictures by Casanova, a brother of the more famous libertine. A small library dating from Louis XIII in 1635 comes next with beautiful leather-bound books, and the floor of diamond shaped tiles, *tomettes,* put in at the same time that the ceiling beams were painted.

History of the Château

Of all the treasures in the Saintonge region none can surely compare to the treasure of **La Roche-Courbon**. Like so many châteaux, it had its origin in the middle ages when the *donjon* was built in 1475. Parts of the *donjon* have been retained in the modern château and the drawbridge, the moats and towers are all in use today. When peace came to the countryside in the mid-1600s the château was altered to a residence and a number of families have occupied it over the years. Among them the de Courbon family, who stayed for 234 years until they sold it in 1817.

The succeeding owners, including a cognac house, neglected it and it fell into ruin, and by the end of the last century it was dilapidated and its lands were overgrown and wild. In 1908 it was suggested that the fabric be sold as building material, and all the woods cut for timber.

Onto the scene came Pierre Loti (see page 100). Loti, a writer of romantic works, had spent many years in the east and delighted in the solitude of La Roche-Courbon. He travelled from Saintes on the tramway to St-Porchaire and walked through the woods to the château.

The overgrown woods, the dilapidated buildings and the general air of decay, made him think of the Sleeping Beauty story, and he began to weave the legend into the architecture and the estate. Today as you approach from St-Porchaire the tall holm oaks overhang the road, and with the deep forests extending far to one side, you can begin to believe that Sleeping Beauty really did live here.

Turn down the drive to park and as you enter the magnificent grounds, you are now convinced that not only would she have chosen a château as beautiful as this, but it is only here that her prince would have expected to find her.

Loti used the legend to stir someone with the means and the ability to rescue this sleeping beauty and restore it to life. His cry was heard by Paul Chénéreau in 1920, who devoted the rest of his 99 years, and the greater part of his fortune to restoring the château and its grounds. Today his grandson Jacques Badois owns the château and with his wife runs it and nearly 750 acres (300 hectares) of land as forest and farm, in particular, making goat's cheese.

As you go into the room traditionally called the Bathroom, it doesn't strike you as having the most suitable name. On all sides are pictures painted on wood panelling; on the walls, on the ceiling, in the window bays. Then as you recover your senses, there it is: the bath, near the door and in an alcove arched with more pictures, this time biblical scenes!

But what a bath! Made of shaped and smoothed limestone blocks there are two holes near the top to allow the water in, and a hole, that one hesitates to call a 'plug hole' in so grand a setting, at the bottom to let it out. How much hot water it contained, how cold the stone blocks must have made it, one can surmise. But what it was like to contemplate biblical scenes while

Château gardens

With the house tour over, you can go into the gardens and admire the symmetrical formality of conical box trees, geometric flower beds, the lake and canals and beyond the lakes the grand staircase that leads to the viewpoint. Do visit this for the best view and best place to photograph the château.

The gardens were restored between 1928 and 1936 to give a typical French formal garden. Originally they had been laid out on the marshy ground that was so important in medieval times as a defensive measure. But now with the disadvantage of no solid ground to a depth of 25ft (8m), each autumn these days, special stakes and floors are inserted so the statues, lawns and paths can be preserved. In fact the landing stage at the north end of the garden is now 5ft (1.5m) below the water level, whereas in 1935 it was 3in (8cm) above.

To the south of the gardens the ornamental gateway and path lead to pre-historic caves by the river about 550yd (500m) away. If you wish to explore the caves themselves, be sure to have a good torch, though this is at your own risk! On the way back you can spot Pierre Loti's name carved in the limestone – by himself or an admirer?

one's servant scrubbed one's back, almost defies imagination!

In the drawing room is a painting of the château as it was in 1660 by the Dutch painter Hackeart. It was used as the guide to restore the gardens in the 1930s. The next two rooms are from the mid-1600s with painted beams and connected by a door that opens itself when knocked upon!

In the first room the magnificent fireplace carries the motto of the de Courbon family *Fide Fidelitate Fortitudine* – Faith Fidelity and Courage. Whilst the second has been set up as a kitchen in the local country style with an old mechanical spit.

On the first floor in the north tower is a typical country bedroom with traditional furniture, including two four poster beds with curtains. Step out onto the balcony to see the charming formal gardens, then

down to the Guard Room that we would now call a summer room. On the level of the gardens, cool in summer and warm in winter, this was the original main entrance with a circular staircase (now lost) leading to the other floors.

SOUTH OF SAINTES

Pons, once a stage on the pilgrim's road to Santiago de Compostella, sits on a hill above the river Seugne and is dominated by a massive square *donjon*. Park under the trees and the Tourist Office is in the *donjon* itself with displays of work by local craft workers.

At the *Hôtel de Ville* just to the right of the *donjon* follow the arrowed walk round the city walls. At the Café Donjon take the Rue Château d'Eau, Water Tower Street, turn right at the little and very pretty passage called Rue du

The Donjon

The Donjon was built around the year 1000 by the Lords of Pons as part of the castle that covered the present public gardens and the car park. Richard the Lion Heart destroyed it in 1178, but it was rebuilt nine years later with walls that are 15ft (4.5m) thick on the northern side and 8ft (2.5m) thick on the others. A staircase leads to the first floor and the Great Hall, 66 x 25 x 49ft high (20 x 7.5 x 15m). The next staircase of 133 steps takes you to the roof and the battlements. The top was reconstructed in 1904 and is 100ft (30m) or so above the gardens below and the view over the town is very pretty.

Robinet, Tap Street, crossing straight into Ruelle des Glycines, Wisteria Lane, dropping you down to the water that you had seen from the walls above.

Wander into the little garden of the Angling Club that occupies the site of the old water mill. Above you are the old walls and the *donjon* and castle, while at your feet is a quiet and peaceful scene by the winding branches of the river and the old *lavoir*, the public wash house. Walk through the pretty little streets of the town before returning to your car. This can take up to another hour.

Turn down the road by the central car park to pick up the signs for **Château d'Usson,** about $1^1/_4$ miles (2km) and over the railway line. This is a pretty, but small renaissance château set in peaceful countryside.

At the end of the last century the original château was located 'two leagues' to the east of Pons, and was moved stone by stone to its present location. The visit allows you to enter the courtyard open on one side and with a view down an avenue of lime trees. The other three sides are highly decorated and inward facing. The Winter Garden occupies the whole of the central portion of the ground floor, with a salon on either side. These two are each partitioned from the winter garden by a plate glass window, giving the viewer an ever-changing picture as the year goes by. Allow three quarters of an hour for your visit.

Winter garden at Château d'Usson

135

COGNAC AND DISTRICT

Cognac is a very popular and busy town so it is best to arrive as early in the day as you can. Depending on how many of the great Cognac houses you wish to visit, you should allow between a half and one day, giving yourself two hours to visit the town.

The old town

In the middle ages Cognac had the monopoly of the local salt trade and imported it up the Charente, therefore the Old Town *(Vieux Cognac)* situated on the hill just below the bridge, has many medieval houses. In 1494 François I was born here. He was one of France's most famous kings, a patron of the arts and scholarship in the Renaissance and a humanist. Watch out for his emblem: the salamander.

The *Chais*, the cognac houses, are mostly by the river around and below the Old Town. The hub of the modern town is away from the river beyond the church, and at the far end is the Place François I.

Nearby in Rue du 14 Juli is the Tourist Office. Although you will want to wander through the streets both old and new, do make sure you also use the main road flanking the west of the middle of town, leading from Place François I to the *Ancien Château* (Otard's Chais). You will pass the Market Hall and the Villa François I, now the Social Security Office, on the town side, and the large Municipal Gardens around the *Hôtel de Ville* and the Musée du Cognac on the other.

The streets of special interest in *Vieux Cognac* include: Grande Rue winding up from the Porte St Jacques on the river to the church of St Leger; Rue de l'Isle d'Or and Rue Saulnier (Salt Merchant Street) with many attractive façades from the sixteenth and seventeenth centuries. Rue du Palais has a former wool carder's house at No. 2, next door a half timbered house of 1374, and beyond that a house of 1373, all in occupation. Leading off all these streets are the most delightful little cobbled lanes, each one asking to be explored.

There are three actual producers with *chais* in Cognac: Otard, Henessey and Martell. Outside the town are Rémy Martin and Prince Hubert de Polignac. Camus in the town is a wholesaler only. All will give conducted tours of their premises, and normally finish with either a miniature or a sample to drink. In the summer months you can expect an English speaking guide to escort you. (see panel for details)

Jarnac is another cognac town, best known for the house of Courvoisier, and as the birth and burial place of President Mitterand. Although not very big it is a pleasing town dominated by its château and the bridge over the Charente. The Tourist Office is near the château, the headquarters of Courvoisier. Go to the entrance near the bridge to take a tour of the *chais* of about an hour.

The other main producer here is Hine whose storage warehouses are on the outskirts of the town towards Angoulême, but whose offices are in Quai L'Orangerie. Not far from them is Delamain et Cie in Rue Delamain, wholesalers, and in Rue Jacques Moreau is A.E. Dor. All three houses will be pleased to supply you with brandy and *Pineau des Charentes*, Jarnac being the leading producer.

You can visit the church where the Lords of Jarnac are buried and in the square is a daily market, larger on Tuesdays and Sundays.

There are plenty of smaller cognac and *pineau* producers, especially along the D731, Cognac to St-Jean-d'Angely road. However at **Migron**, 3km to the east of the road is the Ecomusée at the Logis des Bessons, owned by the Tesseron Family.

This is a family run business in the heart of the country where they make cognac and *pineau* as well as having five *chambres d'hôtes*, bed and breakfast accommodation, and a swimming pool for guests. The family has been

established here for eight generations and everything in their museum has come down from the father to son.

They have set out a number of rooms to explain the life of the cognac producer in the last century: a cooperage room, the press room, the living room with all the furniture, tools, instruments and the like. Then at the back of the building are the *alambics,* stills, used today to produce the cognac from the wine, whilst on show at the front is another one 200 years old.

Naturally you will be able to buy bottles of cognac and *Pineau des Charentes* here, and like many of the other smaller producers, their products are often better value than those of the larger houses.

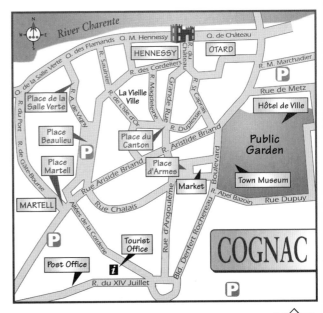

Visits may be made to the following chais:

Henessey, founded by an Irishman, and still owned by the family, has its offices, waiting room and museum on the Cognac side of the river, and its chais on the other joined by a three minute boat trip! ☎ 05 45 35 72 68. Open: March to December 10am-5pm, June to September 6pm, visits also available in the rest of the year.

Martell is the oldest of the great houses dating back to 1715. The tour here includes an audio-visual history of cognac, the chais, the bottling and the packing. ☎ 05 45 36 33 33. Open: July to September, Monday to Friday 9.45am-5pm, weekends 10am-4.15pm, visits also available in the rest of the year.

Camus' visit includes cooperage as well as the making and ageing of cognac. ☎ 05 45 32 28 28. Open: July to October, Monday to Friday, 10am-noon, 2.30pm-4.30pm, visits also available in the rest of the year.

Otard, was founded by a Scot, and uses the old castle of Cognac as its _chais_ with half the visit devoted to the history of the castle. Outside the castle, and on the side facing the river is the 'King's Balcony', sculptured with salamanders. Richard the Lion Heart married his son Phillip to Amélie de Cognac in the ancient Helmet Room, _La Salle au Casque,_ named after the carving of a helmet on the huge fireplace. ☎ 05 45 36 88 86. Open: July and August every half hour 10am-11am, 1.30pm-6pm, visits also available in the rest of the year.

Rémy Martin, only nine years younger than Martell will take you on your visit by a little train to see the largest cooperage in Europe. ☎ 05 45 35 76 66. Open: April to October.

Prince Hubert de Polignac is a co-operative of vine growers founded in 1949, and produces both cognac and _Pineau des Charentes_. ☎ 05 45 32 13 85. Open: July to mid-September 10am, 11am, 2pm, 3pm, 4pm, 5pm. Visits also available in the rest of the year.

The **St Gobain Glass Factory** produces bottles and is open to visitors over the age of 14 years during the summer for a charge. You should book through the Tourist Office.

The production of Cognac

Cognac is made only from the grapes grown in the area around the town, with the most suitable grown on the best chalky soil to the south-east around Segonzac.

This is the Grande Champagne. The name 'Champagne' is used since both the soil and the grape are similar to those in the Champagne area around Rheims and Epernay in the north of France. In descending order of quality and greater distance from Cognac the other areas of vine cultivation are called Petite Champagne, Borderies, Fins Bois, Bons Bois and finally right by the sea Bois Ordinaires.

The leading Cognac Houses tend to use only the first four, since they believe the taste of the sea and more especially the taste of the seaweed used to fertilize the vines in the outer two Bois areas can effect the cognac. In late October and early November the grapes are harvested and fermented quickly.

They must not be allowed to have a second fermentation, so desirable with champagne itself. From December to April the *alambics* distill the spirit. The wine is slightly preheated in the *Chauf Vin* before entering the *Chaudière* over gas flames. It is taken through the Swan's neck to the *Serpentin*, condenser, and the first distillation is collected at about 30 per cent proof.

A second distillation increases the *eau-de-vie* to over 160 per cent proof when it is stored in barrels. Although a minimum of two and a half years is required to produce drinkable cognac, some has been maturing since 1820.

Only oak from the Limousin region of France is used in the barrels as the wood has the best porosity and the right levels of tannin to augment the *eau-de-vie*. Cellar masters taste the cognac from time to time to assess its progress. From their decisions batches are combined to produce one of a number of qualities of cognac.

MUSÉE REGIONAL

Fouras

Open: mid-June to mid-September daily 3pm-6pm, mid-September to mid-June Sundays and holidays same.

THE PALMYRE ZOO

10 miles (16km)
from Royan on the D25.

Allow half day for your visit.
☎ 05 46 22 46 06. Open: daily, April to September 9am-7pm, low season 9am-noon, 2pm-6pm. July to September – bus service from Royan.

CHÂTEAU DE LA GATAUDIÈRE

Near Marennes

☎ 05 46 85 01 07. Open: March to end November 10am-noon, 2pm-6.30pm; closed Mondays, October, November and March to June.

MUSÉE DE LA POCHE DE ROYAN

At the D733 roundabout at Le Gua.
☎ 05 46 22 89 90. Open: daily July to September 10am-7pm, October to June 10am-noon, 2pm-6pm.

ARCHAEOLOGICAL MUSEUM

Saintes

Open: Tuesday to Sunday, summer 10am-noon, 2pm-6pm; winter closes 5.30pm; Sundays 2pm-6pm.

MUSEUM OF PRE-HISTORY

Saintes

Some 440yd (400m) along the Rue Gambetta from the Pont B. Palissy Gives an interesting view of the early life of man. The star exhibit in the garden is an immense stone weighing many tons used by neolithic man who, with sand and water, polished his axes. The grooves he made are clearly visible.
☎ 05 46 93 43 27. 1 hour guided tour. Open: 10am-11.30am, 3pm-5.30pm.

CHÂTEAU DU DOUHET

About 7 miles (11km)
north of Saintes.

The main residential building of the château is facing you as you go through the gateway at the end of the large *Court d'Honneur*. Allow at least an hour and a half for this visit, better still bring a picnic and take half a day.
☎ 05 46 97 78 14. Open: April to October 10am-noon, 2.30pm-7pm, Sundays, bank and school holidays 2.30pm-5.30pm, also November to March.

CHÂTEAU BEAUFIEF

Near St Jean d'Angely

Charming small eighteenth-century manor house. Allow an hour for the visit.
☎ 05 46 32 35 93. Open: daily Easter to Nov 1st 2.30pm-6.30pm.

CHÂTEAU DAMPIERRE-SUR-BOUTONNE

Near Aulnay

The tour is conducted in French with an English résumé available. Allow an hour to include a walk round the small grounds.
☎ 05 46 24 02 24.

Open: 15 June to 15 September daily 10am-noon, 2pm-6.30pm; October, November, Sundays and holidays by appointment 2pm-6pm.

CHÂTEAU DE PANLOY

North-west of Saintes and 3 miles (5km) from Taillebourg.

The visit, with printed guides in English, comprises the house, the dovecote and the stables and laundry. Allow up to an hour.
☎ 05 46 91 73 23.
Open: daily 15 March to 15 September 10am-noon, 2pm-6.30pm; closed Mondays. Also by appointment.

Interior of Château Beaufief

CHÂTEAU DE CRAZANNES

A mile (2km) away from Château de Panloy.

☎ 05 46 90 15 94.
Open: school holidays and every weekend from May to October, 2.30pm-6.30pm. Also by appointment.

THE CHÂTEAU DE LA ROCHE-CORBON

About 1¹/₄ miles (2km) to the north of the main road between Saintes and Rochefort at St-Porchaire.

You can visit the gardens alone or the château and gardens together. Accompanied tours of the château begin about every three quarters of an hour and are in French with a hand-out in English. Allow best part of a day.
☎ 05 46 95 60 10.
e-mail larochecourbon@t3a.com
Open: daily 10am-noon, 2.30pm-6.30pm, winter 5.30pm; closed Thursdays mid-September to mid June and mid-February to mid-March.

DONJON AT PONS

Allow up to 30 minutes. Crafts for sale.
☎ 05 46 91 46 46.
Open: 15 June to 15 September, 9am-noon, 2pm-7pm.

L'ECOMUSÉE DU COGNAC

☎ 05 46 94 19 16. Open: June to September 10am-12.30pm, 2.30pm-6.30pm.

Fact File

GETTING THERE

From England

If you are travelling from England, the easiest routes by car and ferry are from Portsmouth to St Malo by Brittany Ferries, or from Poole to St Malo by Condor Ferries; Portsmouth to Cherbourg by P&O Ferries, or Portsmouth to Caen by Brittany Ferries,

The distances from these ports to la Roche-sur-Yon, departmental capital of the Vendée is St Malo: 149 miles (240km); Cherbourg: 239 miles (385km); Caen: 214 miles (345km).

From St Malo the N137 goes direct to Rennes and Nantes, where the A83 autoroute (motorway) and D763 expressway will take you to la Roche-sur-Yon. Leaving Cherbourg, the N13/N174 go to St Lô where take A84 for Rennes, the rest of the journey as for St Malo. Arrival at Caen offers a speedy journey: N175 expressway A84 autoroute for Rennes, travel on as above.

By car in France

To the north of the region

The quickest route for the Vendée and the Pays de Retz from Paris, is along the A11 autoroute (motorway) via Le Mans and Angers to Nantes. From the Nantes ring road, *périphérique*, take the D751 for the Pays de Retz and the Ile de Noirmoutier

For the northern Vendéen resorts, from the ring road take the A83, and at the first exit, no.1, take the D937/D262.

For the southern resorts, leave the A83 autoroute at exit 4, take the D763 expressway to La Roche-sur-Yon and from the ring road take the N160 expressway to Les Sables-d'Olonne.

To the south of the region

You can reach the area by car along the Paris – Bordeaux A10 autoroute.

Exit 32 serves Niort itself, and for the southern Vendéen coastal resorts and the Marais Poitevin, follow the Niort by-pass take the N148/D949.

If you are making for La Rochelle use exit 33, and the N11 expressway will take to the city centre and the Ile de Ré.

Leave the A10 at St-Jean-d'Angely, exit 34, for Rochefort by leaving the A10 at Saintes, exit 35, you have a direct route via N150 to Royan, or take the N150/D728 to Ile d'Oléron. This exit also serves Cognac via the Saintes ring-road, *pérépherique* and N147.

For details of maps available and how to get them, see the section below.

By Rail

The Eurostar service from Waterloo Station in London arrives at the

Gare du Nord in Paris. SNCF, the French railway company, runs the 'TGV Atlantique' the very fast express train that leaves Paris Gare Montparnasse for la Rochelle (☎ 08 36 35 35 35, or 08 36 35 35 39 in English). This service is first class only, and at between 3 and 4 hours journey time is much speedier than the normal express trains, which leave from Paris Gare d'Austerlitz, same phone number.

By Air

There is a frequent air service from Gatwick (England) to Nantes, (UK ☎ 0208 742 6600) though you will need to fly into Paris for the nearest inter-continental routes. From Paris Orly, Air-Inter flies to la Rochelle (☎ 05 46 42 30 26).

GETTING ABOUT

Driving

Speed limits:	**Dry roads**	*Wet roads*
Built-up area	**50kmph** (31mph)	*50kmph*
Single carriage way main roads	**90kmph** (56mph)	*80kmph (50mph)*
Dual carriageway main roads	**110kmph** (68mph)	*100kmph (62mph)*
Motorways	**110-130kmph** (68-81mph)	*110kmph*
Motorways minimum speed	**50kmph**	*50kmph*

50kmph on all roads when visibility is reduced below 50 metres (approx 50 yards).

Parking

French towns and cities are blessed with many car parks, charged for in the larger towns and normally free in the smaller. Parking is allowed on the road where indicated. Make sure you are facing the direction of the traffic and that you are aware of any restrictions. Many towns allow parking on one side of the street from the 1st of the month to the 15th, and the other side from the 16th to 31st.

In this rural area you will normally have little trouble parking, and where advice needs to be given for a particular town or resort, you will find it in the text.

Documents and special equipment

Take with you your driving licence, car registration document or hire certificate, proof of insurance and a European Accident Statement.

You will need a warning triangle and a set of spare bulbs. A first aid kit and two external rear-view mirrors are recommended. Motorcyclists must wear a safety helmet.

Fact File

Seat belts and child safety

Seat belts must be used where fitted and worn at all times. The minimum age for a child in the front seat is 10 years. However, children under this age may be carried here so long as an approved seat is used and faces backwards. Children under 9 months may be carried the same way in the rear, though those up to 4 years must have a child safety seat. Those between 5 and 10 years may use a booster seat.

Rule of the Road

Drive on the right, overtake on the left. Away from main roads, beware traffic entering from the right, they have the right of way. Roundabouts in the country have priority for those on the round-about, in towns the opposite is true, but be sure to read any signs. Traffic signals are smaller and less bright than UK and Eire, attention is needed! Watch the lower, repeater, signals on your right if you stop by the lights.

Emergencies

Dial 17 for police, 18 for fire, *pompiers*, 15 for SAMU, paramedics. All motorways have roadside emergency phones, and many main roads have orange roadside emergency phones every $1^1/_4$ miles (2km) or phone the local Gendarmerie (police).

Car Hire

Car hire is available at all airports mentioned, and at la Rochelle railway station. Hertz, central reservation ☎ 01 47 88 51 51, Avis, central reservation ☎ 01 46 10 60 60, and local companies all offer services from leading garages, as well as their own offices.

Buses

Long distance services from Paris serve the region, but you will probably make more use of the city bus services in la Rochelle, Niort and la Roche-sur-Yon. There are infrequent country services.

• GENERAL INFORMATION •

ACCOMODATION AND EATING OUT

(Herbergement et Restuaration)

This is one of the major holiday areas of France, with many hundreds of hotels, bed and breakfast (*chambres d'hôtes*) holiday cottages (*gîtes*) and camp sites; restaurants, cafés, bistros and ethnic res-taurants. To list any of these in a guide of this size would be both random and subjective.

On page 152 you will find a list of the major Tourist Offices, and all have English speaking staff. On request by phone, letter or personal call, they will supply you with a comprehensive booklet of accommodation and eating houses in their area.

ANNUAL EVENTS IN THE REGION

These are the main events but there are many more local events over the year and details of these will be found in the tourist offices and local advertising.

Cognac

April	An international Festival of Detective Films
September-October	Celebration of the Grape Harvest and Flower Festival in alternate years.

Luçon

Second Saturday in July	Concert and theatre in the Jardin Dumaine
Second weekend in August	Fair and exhibitions

Melle

Late May to mid-June	Music Festival
July	Goats' Cheese Festival

Le Puy-du-Fou

Mid-June to early September	Cinéscénie spectacular light and sound show.

La Rochelle

Weekend and week before Whitsun	International sailing week.
Around 14 July	Festival of French songs from around the globe: FrancoFolies.

Saintes

Around 14 July	International Folk Festival and Music Festival.

St-Jean-Croix-de-Vie

August	Onion Fair

La Tranche-sur-Mer

From April	Flower Festival

CREDIT AND DEBIT CARDS AND MONEY

Most credit cards are accepted in most businesses, hotels, super-markets and on the autoroutes for payment of tolls. It is advisable to

Above: Barbâtre: cottage, Noitmoutier

Right: Zoo at Palmyre

Below: A Bar in St-Jean-de-Monts

Above: Sunflowers
Below: Place Belliard, Fontenay-le-Comte

know and have ready your PIN number, as this is occasionally required. See though, the notes under petrol stations in supermarkets.

Debit and credit cards can be used to access cash at most cash points in banks throughout France, where the instructions are multi-lingual. You must report any loss of a debit or credit card to the police who will issue you with a certificate.

Travellers' cheques are widely accepted, but you can expect a fairly stiff charge for changing them in many banks. Better to take these valued in French francs and find a bank that does not charge. A passport is required when cashing travellers' cheques. Eurocheques are also in use.

Banks open from 9am to noon and from 2pm to 4pm, closing on either Monday or Saturday. There is no restriction on the import or export of French and other currency for holiday purposes, though there are some restrictions on the export of large quantities of cash.

The French Franc is the unit of currency, divided into 100 centimes. Most prices in shops and hotels are quoted in francs and euros, which will supersede the franc during 2002.

ELECTRICITY

This region of France is at 220 volts ac 50 hertz. You will need an adapter plug for the French two pin system.

EMBASSIES

United Kingdom
35, Rue du Faubourg Saint-Honoré, 75008 Paris.
☎ 01 44 51 31 00.

Republic of Ireland
4 Rue Rude, 75016 Paris.
☎ 01 44 17 67 00.

USA
2 Avenue Gabrielle, 75382 Paris.
☎ 01 43 12 22 22.

Canada
35/37 Avenue Montaigne, 75008, Paris.
☎ 01 44 43 29 00

FRENCH GOVERNMENT TOURIST OFFICES

Great Britain
178 Picadilly, London WV1 0AL,
☎ 0891 244 123,
Fax 0207 493 6594.
www.piccadilly@mdlf.demon.co.uk

Ireland
10 Suffolk Street, Dublin 2.
☎ 01 679 0813, Fax: 01 679 0814, internet as GB.

USA
444 Madison Avenue, 16th Fl., New York, NY, 10022 – 2452.
☎ 212 838 7800,
Fax: 212 838 7855.
www.info@francetourism.com

Canada
30, St Patrick Street, Suite 700, Toronto, ONT, M5T 3A3.
☎ 416 – 593 4723,
Fax: 416 – 979 7587.
www.frenchtourist@sympatico.ca

HEALTH

Reciprocal state health care is available for UK and Irish residents
holidaying in France. You will need a form E111, obtained by
completing the form at the back of the booklet 'Health Advice for
Travellers' from Post Offices or by phoning (UK) ☎ 0800 555777,
and taking it to a Post Office for stamping. This should not preclude
UK and Irish residents from taking out personal medical insurance.

Travellers from other countries should check with their own
insurers for validity in France.

Pharmacies are easily seen with their green crosses, often in neon.
Here they will deal with minor ailments, and advise if and where
more treatment is needed.

HOURS OF BUSINESS

These are somewhat different to those obtaining in the United
Kingdom and other English speaking countries. Most shops and
businesses open from around 9am to between noon and 1pm when
they close for up to two hours, though most re-open between 2pm
and 2.30pm. Shops will stay open until as late as 8pm, but 6pm or
7pm are more usual.

Supermarkets :

Generally stay open all day in their larger branches, though all will
close on Mondays in common with most other shops. Bakers and
newsagents open every day including Sunday morning and sometimes
a local supermarket might do the same.

Petrol stations :

Will follow the local shop hours, especially if they are tied to a
supermarket. However, many supermarkets allocate one or more
petrol pumps to payment direct by credit or debit card. You will need
to use your PIN number, but you cannot be certain this will always
work with a foreign card. It is safer to pay at the kiosk!

Markets :

You need to get up early for the best bargains at a French market.
They will start as early as 6am, though 7am and 8am are more
common. By lunch time, noon, the stall holders will all be packing up
and are very reluctant to do business.

Places to visit :

The times and dates of opening of the major attractions are shown in
each entry, however, for other smaller attractions not listed, a
working assumption that they open from 10am to noon and 2pm to
6pm during the holiday season will be useful.

Fact File

LANGUAGE

English is spoken in all the main tourist offices, and in a number of the less important, as well as hotels and a few large stores. However the ability to speak a foreign language is not usually admitted to by French people, and you will need to have at least a smattering of French. A good phrase book will be invaluable, such as those by Berlitz or Hugo, and a few hours spent practising with a tape or CD before you leave will repay you many times over.

MAPS

Michelin: 1:200,000 1cm to 2km, or about 3 miles to the inch, numbers 232 and 233 cover the area, or current year's Road Atlas at same scale

IGN (French 'Ordnance Survey' or 'USGS'): 1:100,000 1cm to 1km, numbers 32 and 33 for the Vendée, and 39 for the Marais Poitevin, La Rochelle and Charente will give the detail needed to reach many of the places mentioned. ($1^1/_4$ inches to 2 miles, very approximately)

IGN: 1:25,000 ($2^1/_2$ inches to the mile [4cm to 1km]) for the islands: Ile Noirmoutier number 1125OT, Ile de Ré 1329OT, Ile d'Oléron 1330OT, will repay their cost if you are spending time on any of them.

Where to buy IGN maps

There are over 100 specialist map shops and bookshops with a specialist map department in the UK who carry a stock. You are less likely to find them in large multiples. In case of difficulty, contact **Hereford Map Centre**, Map House, 24/25 Church Street, Hereford, HR1 2LR, ☎ 01432 266322, Fax: 01432 341874, e-mail mapped@globalnet.co.uk. where all the maps mentioned are stocked. They are available from good bookshops in France.

NEWSPAPERS

In this region, English newspapers are normally available in the larger towns the day after publication in the UK. The European edition of the *International Herald Tribune* is published in France and is also available in the larger towns on the day of publication.

Le Monde and *Le Figaro* are French language papers roughly equivalent to the British *Times* or the *Daily Telegraph*. *L'Equippe* is the sporting newspaper. However more important for local news and events is *Ouest France* which covers this area.

PASSPORTS, VISAS AND CUSTOMS

Passports are required for visitors from the UK, Ireland, the USA and Canada, but visas are not required.

UK and Irish travellers have few restrictions on the import and export of normal holiday purchases such as alcoholic drink, tobacco and gifts, being both in the EU. For travellers from the USA and Canada, there are restrictions, and readers should acquaint themselves with the current regulations before leaving, www.info@francetourism.com.

POSTING LETTERS HOME AND USING THE TELEPHONE

Stamps, *timbres de post*, are available from post offices and cafés who also sell tobacco, *bureaux de tabac,* which all have a red double cone above the entrance. Post offices in large cities and towns are open all day, but in smaller towns follow local custom by closing for a couple of hours in the middle of the day. (see Hours of Business).

If you intend phoning home often, it is best to buy a *télécarte*, again available from *bureaux de tabac*, newsagents and post offices. You may prefer, in the UK, to have a BT Chargecard with an international facility, where you will speak to a UK operator and call charges are made to your own telephone account. Similar arrangements can be made in Ireland, the USA, and Canada. Mobile phones can also be compatible for use abroad, though the call charges are high.

Codes to Great Britain are 19, pause and wait for next dialling tone, 44.

Ireland 19, pause and wait for next dialling tone, 353

USA and Canada 19, pause and wait for next dialling tone, 1

Remember to omit any initial 0 in the home country code.

PUBLIC HOLIDAYS

Museums almost always close on these days, as do shops and offices.

January 1st	New Year's Day *(Jour de l'An)*
Easter Day and Easter Monday	*(Pâques)*
Whit Sunday and Monday	*(Pentecôte)*
Ascension Day	*(Ascension)*
July 14	Bastille Day
August 15	Assumption *(l'Assomption)*
November 1st	All Saints' Day *(Toussaints)*
November 11	Armistice Day
25 December	Christmas Day *(Noël)*

Fact File

TIME

France is one hour ahead of Greenwich Mean Time (GMT) except between the end of September and the end of October, when it is the same. When it is noon in France it is: 11am in London and Dublin, 6am in New York and 3am in Los Angeles. The 24-hour clock is in use: eg. 1.30pm becomes *13.30*, 8pm is *20.00 heures*.

TIPPING

Most menus are designated *'service complet'* meaning tips are included, though you may wish to add extra at the end of your meal. It is usual to tip a tourist guide, the usherette in a cinema and taxi drivers.

TOURIST OFFICES

Smaller offices are mentioned in the text.

When phoning from the UK, precede these numbers by 0033 and omit the initial 0

Charente-Maritime Tourist Board, Departmental Office. BP 58 17003 la Rochelle, Cedex 1. ☎ 05 46 44 29 52 Fax 05 46 44 70 10, www.france-atlantique.com, e-mail: tourisme.larochelle@wanadoo. fr (note: not town of Cognac).

Vendee Tourist Board, Departmental Office. 8, Place Napoléon, BP 233, 85006 La Roche-sur-Yon Cedex. ☎ 02 51 47 88 22 for brochures.

Bretignolles-sur-Mer, 85470, BP 10, 1 Bvd du Nord, ☎ 02 51 90 12 78, Fax 02 51 22 40 72.

Cognac, 16112. 16 Rue 14 Juillet, BP 247. ☎ 05 45 82 10 71, Fax 05 45 82 34 47, e-mail office.tourisme.cognac@wanadoo.fr

Fontenay-le-Comte, 85200, Tour d'Octroi, ☎ 02 51 69 44 99. **Fouras,** 17450, BP 32. ☎ 05 46 84 60 69, Fax 05 46 84 28 04, www.fouras.net.

Ile de Noirmoutier, 85330, Route du Pont, ☎ 02 51 39 80 71, Fax: 02 51 39 53 16. www.île-noirmoutier.com.fr

Ile d'Oléron and Marennes, 17560 Bourcefranc. ☎ 05 46 85 65 23, Fax 05 46 85 68 96, www.ot-chateau-oleron.fr, e-mail chatolero@ot-chateau-oleron.fr

Ile de Ré, 17580, BP 28, Le-Bois-Plage. ☎ 05 46 09 00 55, Fax 05 46 09 00 54, e-mail ilederetourisme@wanadoo.fr

La Faute-sur-Mer, 85460, Rond-Point Fleuri, ☎ 02 51 56 45 19, Fax 02 51 97 18 08.

La Rochelle, 17025. Place de la Petite Sirène, Le Gabut, CEDEX. ☎ 05 46 41 14 68, Fax 05 46 41 99 85, www.ville-larochelle.fr, e-mail tourism.larochelle@wanadoo.fr

La Roche-sur-Yon, 85000, Rue du Georges Clemenceau, ☎ 02 51 36 00 85, Fax 02 51 47 56 57.

La Tranche-sur-Mer, 85360, Place de la Liberté, ☎ 02 51 30 33 96, Fax 02 51 27 78 71.

Les Sables-d'Olonne, 85104, Centre de Congrès, ☎ 02 51 96 85 85, Fax 02 51 96 85 71, www.ot-lessablesdolonne.fr

Luçon, 85402, Square Eduard Herriot, BP 269 Cedex. ☎ 02 51 56 36 52, Fax 02 51 56 03 56.

Melle, 79500, 3 Rue Emilion Taver, BP 51, ☎ 05 49 29 15 10, Fax 05 49 29 19 83.

Niort, 79008, Rue Ernest Pérochon, BP 277, ☎ 05 49 24 18 79, Fax: 05 49 24 98 90, www.ot-niort-paysniortaisepoitevin.fr

Notre-Dame-de-Monts, 85690, Route de la Barre, ☎ 02 51 58 84 97, Fax 02 51 58 15 65.

Pornic, 44210, La Gare, Tel 02 40 82 40 02, Fax 02 40 82 90 12.

Rochefort, 17300, Avenue Sadi Carnot, also Porte de l'Arsenal. ☎ 05 46 99 18 60, Fax 05 46 99 52 64. www.ville-rochefort.fr e-mail maire@ville-rochefort.fr

Royan, 17207. Le Front, BP138, CEDEX. ☎ 05 46 05 04 71, Fax 05 46 06 67 76.

Saintes, 17103. Villa Musso, 62 Cours National, BP 96. ☎ 05 46 74 23 82, Fax 05 46 92 17 01, e-mail saintongetour@wanadoo.fr.

Saint-Jean-d'Angely, 17400, 8 Rue de la Grosse Horlorge, ☎ 05 46 32 04 72.

St-Gilles-Croix-de-Vie, 85800, Bvd de l'Egalité, BP 57, ☎ 02 51 55 03 66, Fax 02 51 55 69 60.

WINE

There is little wine produced in the area covered by this guide. However there are a few areas, notably in the south of the Vendée, and these are all mentioned in the text along with a selection of producers. The wine is described as being VDQS. This is the second highest wine classification and stands for: *vins délimités de qualité supérieure.* The nearest wine areas carrying the highest classification of AOC, *appellation d'origine controlée,* is in the Loire Valley, to the north and the Bordeaux region to the south.

The large vineyards around Cognac produce wine solely for the production of cognac itself and *Pineau des Charentes.* A full description of the grapes and production of cognac and *Pineau* is given in the Cognac section.

LANDMARK VISITORS GUIDES

US & British VI*
ISBN: 1 901522 03 2
256pp,
UK £11.95 US $15.95

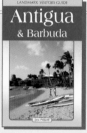

Antigua & Barbuda*
ISBN: 1 901522 02 4
96pp,
UK £5.95 US $12.95

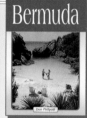

Bermuda*
ISBN: 1 901522 07 5
160pp,
UK £7.95 US $12.95

Barbados*
ISBN: 1 901522 32 6
160pp,
UK £7.95 US $12.95

Dominican Republic*
ISBN: 1 901522 08 3
160pp,
UK £7.95 US $12.95

Cayman Islands*
ISBN: 1 901522 33 4
160pp
UK £7.95 US $12.95

Gran Canaria*
ISBN: 1 901522 19 9
112pp
UK £6.50 US $12.95

Jamaica*
ISBN: 1 901522 31 8
160pp
UK £7.95 US $12.95

New Zealand*
ISBN: 1 901522 36 9
320pp
UK £12.95 US $18.95

North Cyprus
ISBN: 1 901522 51 2
192pp
UK £8.95

Ticino
ISBN: 1 901522 74 1
192pp
UK £8.95

Orlando*
ISBN: 1 901522 22 9
256pp,
UK £9.95 US $15.95

Florida: Gulf Coast*
ISBN: 1 901522 01 6
160pp
UK £7.95 US $12.95

Florida: The Keys*
ISBN: 1 901522 21 0
160pp,
UK £7.95 US $12.95

St Lucia*
ISBN: 1 901522 82 2
144pp,
UK £6.95 US $13.95

Provence*
ISBN: 1 901522 45 8
240pp,
UK £10.95 US $17.95

Côte d'Azur*
ISBN: 1 901522 29 6
144pp,
UK £6.95 US $13.95

Dordogne
ISBN: 1 901522 67 9
224pp,
UK £11.95

Italian Lakes*
ISBN: 1 901522 11 3
240pp,
UK £11.95 US $15.95

Pack
2 months
into
2 weeks
with your
Landmark
Visitors
Guides

Bruges*
ISBN: 1 901522 66 0
96pp,
UK £5.95

Riga*
ISBN: 1 901522 59 8
160pp,
UK £7.95

Cracow
ISBN: 1 901522 54 7
160pp,
UK £7.95

Iceland*
ISBN: 1 901522 68 7
192pp,
UK £9.95

Madeira
ISBN: 1 901522 42 3
192pp,
UK £8.95

Tenerife
ISBN: 1 901522 17 2
160pp,
UK £7.95

Languedoc
ISBN: 1 901522 79 2
144pp,
UK £7.95

Sri Lanka
ISBN: 1 901522 37 7
192pp,
UK £9.95

India: Kerala
ISBN: 1 901522 16 4
256pp,
UK £10.99

India: Goa
ISBN: 1 901522 23 7
160pp,
UK £7.95

Prices subject to alteration from time to time

INDEX

LANDMARK

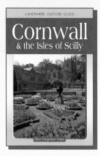

Cornwall
ISBN: 1 901522 09 1
256pp, £9.95

Devon
ISBN: 1 901522 42 3
224pp, £9.95

Dorset
ISBN: 1 901522 46 6
240pp, £9.95

Somerset
ISBN: 1 901522 40 7
224pp, £10.95

Cotswolds
ISBN: 1 901522 12 1
224pp, £9.99

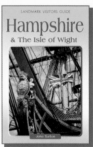

Hampshire
ISBN: 1 901522 14 8
224pp, £9.95

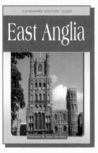

East Anglia
ISBN: 1 901522 58 X
224pp, £9.95

Scotland
ISBN: 1 901522 18 0
288pp, £11.95

Jersey
ISBN: 1 901522 47 4
224pp, £9.99

Guernsey
ISBN: 1 901522 48 2
224pp, £9.95

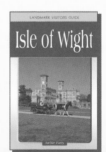

Isle of Wight
ISBN: 1 901522 71 7
112pp, £6.50

VISITORS GUIDES
TO THE UK

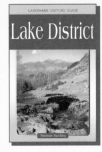

Lake District
ISBN: 1 901522 38 5
224pp, £9.95

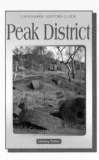

Peak District
ISBN: 1 901522 25 3
240pp, £9.99

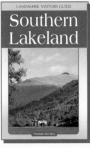

Southern Lakeland
ISBN: 1 901522 53 9
96pp, £5.95

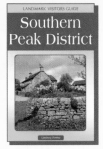

Southern Peak
ISBN: 1 901522 27 X
96pp, £5.95

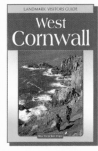

West Cornwall
ISBN: 1 901522 24 5
96pp, £5.95

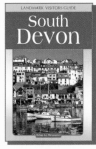

South Devon
ISBN: 1 901522 52 0
96pp, £5.95

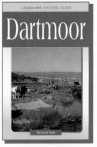

Dartmoor
ISBN: 1 901522 69 5
96pp, £5.95

New Forest
ISBN: 1 901522 70 9
96pp, £5.95

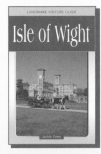

Isle of Wight
ISBN: 1 901522 71 7
96pp, £5.95

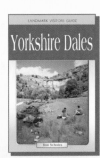

Yorkshire Dales
ISBN: 1 901522 41 5
224pp, £9.95

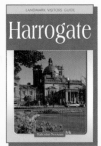

Harrogate
ISBN: 1 901522 55 5
96pp, £4.95

For our address see page 155

Published by
Landmark Publishing Ltd,
Waterloo House, 12 Compton, Ashbourne, Derbyshire DE6 1DA England
Tel: (01335) 347349 Fax: (01335) 347303 e-mail: landmark@clara.net
web site: www.landmarkpublishing.co.uk

1st Edition
ISBN 1 901 522 76 8

British Library Cataloguing in Publication Data: a catalogue record for this book is available from the British Library.

Print: Gutenberg Press Ltd, Malta
Design & Cartography: James Allsopp
Editor: Kay Coulson **Proofreader:** Tim Rose

Front cover: Château de la Roche-Caurbon
Back cover, top: Place Belliard, Fontenay-le-Comte
Back cover, bottom: Fort de l'An Mil, Puy du Fou

Picture Credits:

Association du Puy du Fou: p50
La Rochelle Tourist Office: p83B
La Rochelle Aquarium - photos Lestrade: p86T
Rochefort Tourist Office: p99
All other photographs are supplied by the author.